£10 95

James K Morton

an introduction to
PASCAL

Business Education Publishers Limited

1993

This book is dedicated to my wife, Joan, who is an eternal source
of encouragement and support in all aspects of my life.

© JAMES K MORTON 1993

ISBN 0 907679 47 1

First published in 1993
   Reprinted 1994
   Reprinted 1997
   Reprinted 1999

Cover design by Caroline White

Published in Great Britain by Business Education Publishers Limited,
The Teleport, Doxford International, Sunderland,
Tyne & Wear SR3 3XD
Tel: 0191 525 2400   Fax: 0191 520 1815

British Cataloguing-in-Publications Data
A catalogue record for this book is available from the British Library

Printed by Athenæum Press Ltd, Gateshead, Tyne & Wear

Preface

This book has been specially designed for those studying Pascal for the first time and assumes no prior knowledge of programming. The format of the book provides the student with a logical, step-by-step learning experience proven to be successful in practice.

The material included covers the programming requirements of BTEC National and First Award, City & Guilds Modular Courses and GCE Advanced Level Computing syllabuses. BTEC National/First Award and City & Guilds students will find their requirements met by the material contained in chapters 1 to 5; Advanced Level students should include chapter 6 in their course of study.

Undergraduate and HNC/HND students requiring a working knowledge of Pascal will find this an invaluable text. Chapters 1 to 5 provide the material necessary for a good, general understanding of the Pascal language and chapter 6 provides a platform for those students intending to pursue programming at a professional level.

The book contains a wealth of complete, ready-to-run programs along with numerous end-of-chapter practice programs, exercises and assignments designed to enhance understanding of the material presented in each chapter.

Acknowledgements

This book has been produced with the help of a number of people who deserve particular mention. Special thanks go to Nick Waites, who patiently read and commented upon the first draft of the material, and to Geoff Knott whose encouragement prompted me to write this book.

My thanks go to all at Business Education Publishers and especially to Gareth Dowell who produced the book and Andy Wynd who designed the cover.

Durham
May 1993
JKM

The Author

James K. Morton is a Lecturer in Computing at New College Durham. He has taught Pascal programming for many years on various computing courses including BTEC, City & Guilds and GCE Advanced Level. Prior to entering teaching, he was employed as an engineer in the Computing industry.

Table of Contents

Chapter 1   Fundamentals

Chapter 2   Control Statements

Chapter 3   *Arrays*

Chapter 4   *Functions and Procedures*

Chapter 5   *Files*

Chapter 6   *Advanced Topics*

Chapter 1

Fundamentals

Introduction to the Pascal Programming Language

The Pascal language was introduced in 1971 by Professor Niklaus Wirth of Switzerland. Pascal is a *high level language*, which is a type of programming language intended to be quite easy for people to understand and master. A high level language is really just a special or stylized form of English. This means that a high level language is not very easy for a computer to understand because computers cannot understand English (or any other *natural* language such as French, Italian or German), they can only deal with programs and data that are written in binary form, that is, programs written as strings of 1's and 0's. A program that is in the form that a computer can run (or *execute*) is called a machine code program or, more usually, just *machine code*. It is worth noting that in the early days of computing, programmers had to write their programs in binary form; this turned out to be a task far too difficult and error-prone and so the high level language was invented.

As programmers, however, we need not concern ourselves too much with how a computer is going to understand the programs we write. That has been taken care of already; pieces of software (or programs) exist which can convert our Pascal programs into a form that a computer can understand. These so-called *translation* programs are called *compilers*.

Pascal is a very popular language. It was intended to be easy to learn and use and was designed especially for students. These aims have been achieved with the result that Pascal is now widely available on all types of computers from large mainframes down to personal computers. Today, Pascal is used by professional programmers as well as by students, and complete programming *environments* are now available to make the task of program writing easier. Such an environment consists of a compiler, an editor, debugging aids and various other utilities. The most popular version, or dialect, of Pascal available on personal computers is Turbo Pascal.

Pascal is a language which allows and encourages programmers to write their programs in a manner which makes them logical, easy to understand and easy to maintain. In other words, when learning Pascal, the student is automatically learning good programming habits.

As a programming language, Pascal is essentially a means of giving instructions to a computer and a Pascal program is a set of these instructions, which ultimately, will make a computer perform a particular task or process. (Remember that a Pascal program must be compiled into machine code before it can be run.) The best way to learn to write these instructions, or stated differently, to learn how to program a computer, is to look at lots of programs that have already been written. Having studied them and, hopefully, understood them, the next step is to play around with them by modifying them so that they behave slightly differently (or break down completely!). When confident enough the beginner can begin to devise his or her own programs.

Students of programming need to develop patience. Programs will not normally work first time. The reason for this lies in the nature of the compiler. As stated earlier, a high level language is a special or highly stylized form of English; it is a form of English which has very precise rules of grammar. These rules dictate how we must write down our programming statements. Natural English is noted for having more exceptions to the rules than rules themselves! A compiler is written to understand the limited set of rules which govern the use of a programming language. If the rules are not obeyed completely then the program cannot be translated into machine code and therefore the computer cannot run it. Simply missing out one semi-colon or comma can render a huge program inoperative.

Newcomers to programming should not feel disheartened if their programs fail to work or do not work very well to start with. One of the best 'laws' of programming that I have come across is the one that states 'If a program works first time then it must be useless'. Only the very simplest of programs can be written 'on the spot' without errors. Programmers refer to these errors as *bugs*. It is possible to write programs very quickly, but *debugging* these programs, that is, getting them to run correctly by removing the bugs, takes much, much longer.

The Structure of a Pascal Program

All Pascal programs comply with the format below:

```
program name (input, output);
{Data declarations, if any, go here}

begin
{Main body of program}
{Processing statements go here}
end.
```

Every Pascal program begins with the word *program* and this is followed by the name of the program. Directly after the program name, in brackets, are the words *input* and *output*. This tells Pascal that any input to the program, that is, data fed into it, will come from the standard input device; this will normally be the keyboard. Any output from the program will be written to the standard output device; this will normally be the monitor (or vdu screen). Later, we will see how data can be input and output using devices other than the keyboard and monitor. (See section on files.)

Please note that the word *name*, in the previous program, is shown in bold type. From now on, where a word is shown in bold type it means that it is a *stand-in*. In an actual program the stand-in word would be replaced by some appropriate word that the programmer has chosen. In the program below, **name** has been replaced by the word *simple*. Thus, the program's name is *simple*.

The program below is designed to print out the message 'Hello, is there anyone out there?' onto the monitor. Notice how it follows the program structure shown above.

```
program simple (output);     {Simple demonstration program.}

begin
     writeln('Hello, is there anyone out there?');
end.
```

The program does not require any input from the keyboard while it is running and so the word *input* can be omitted from within the brackets following the program name. The word *output* must remain, of course, because the program is designed to output the message 'Hello, is there anyone out there?' onto the monitor.

The program does not require any data declarations (these will be discussed in the next section) and so the next line contains the word *begin*. This word informs Pascal that the actual instructions to perform some processing will begin at this point. The next line is an instruction to output the message onto the monitor (a later section will discuss this fully) and the final line contains the word *end* followed by a full stop which marks the end of the program. Every Pascal program finishes with the word *end* followed by a full stop.

There are a number of things worth mentioning at this point.

(1)   There are certain words that can be used only as Pascal intends them to be used; these include *reserved words* and *standard identifiers*. The words *program, begin* and *end* are examples of reserved words and the words *output* and *writeln* are examples of standard identifiers. They should not be used for any other purpose.

(2)   Pascal does not distinguish between upper and lower case characters. Thus, the identifier *writeln*, could just as easily be written as *WRITELN* or *WriteLn*. A good policy, however, is to use lower case letters predominantly, as in the program above, because programs tend to look neater that way; capital letters should be used sparingly and for effect only. More will be said about this later.

(3)   Blank lines, spaces and indentations should be used freely to improve the appearance of programs and make them easier to read. Readability is an important property for a program to possess, especially if someone other than the program author has to understand, and perhaps modify, a program.

(4)   Correct punctuation is crucial. Normally, each statement is terminated with a semi-colon; certain words, such as *begin* do not need to be followed by semi-colons because they are not statements. (Look at the previous program.) *Begin*, for example, is a word which marks the beginning of a set or *block* of statements.

(5)   Comments are an important part of any program because they can be used to clarify parts of a program, not just for other people, but also for the program author; a program written even just a few days ago will be so much easier to understand and work on if it contains good comments. Comments are placed inside braces, that is,{ and } or between the compound symbols (* and *); in this text braces will be used throughout. A comment is shown in the first line of the program above. Comments are included for the programmer's use only; they are ignored by the compiler.

Data Types, Constants and Variables

Programs operate on data. For instance, a program could be written to calculate the VAT to be charged on items purchased from a shop; the prices of the items, the items themselves and the rate of value added tax (VAT) are all examples of data. Pascal requires that the types of data to be used in a program must be declared before any processing of the data is done. These *data declarations* are placed at the start of the program before the main body of the program begins. (Refer to the section 'The Structure of a Pascal program'). Note that the main body of a program is placed between the reserved words *begin* and *end*.

Data used by a program is stored in *variables* and *constants*. Variables are used to hold data which can be changed or varied by a program; constants are used to hold data which are never changed by a program. An error will result if a program tries to change the value of a constant. Variables and constants are, in reality, locations in the computer's memory. Thankfully, programmers don't have to keep track of where these locations are in order to refer to them in a program. Variables and constants are given *names* by the programmer, who can then refer to them to by using these names. Variable and constant names are called *identifiers*.

Pascal contains several built-in or standard *data types* for variables; for the present it is sufficient to consider only the data types *integer* and *real*.

Integer Variables

An integer variable is used to store whole numbers only, for example 456 or –34, and these integers must normally lie in the range –32768 to +32767. The reason for these limits is that integers are usually stored using just two bytes of memory (16 bits), along with the 2's complement method for representing negative and positive numbers. The largest positive integer (i.e. 32767) can be referred to in a Pascal program by using the standard identifier *maxint*.

Real Variables

A real variable, on the other hand, can store numbers with or without decimal fraction parts, for example 34.678,–5678 and 0.0123. Real numbers are stored using floating point form and different versions of Pascal use varying amounts of bytes to store these numbers; as an example, Turbo Pascal uses six bytes to store a floating point number, giving the range -10^{38} to 10^{38}.

Variables are declared in a Pascal program by using the word *var* followed by the name (or identifier) and type of each variable.

Constants do not need to have data types associated with them; they are simply declared to have a certain value. The word *const* is used followed by each constant identifier and its value.

The format for declaring data in a Pascal program is as follows:

```
program name (input, output);
const
{Constant declarations go here}
var
{Variable declarations go here}
begin
{The main body of the program goes here}
end.
```

Note that constants must be declared before variables.

The format of each *constant* declaration is

ConstantName = value;

and for each *variable* declaration is

VariableName : DataType;

The program below shows how data declarations are incorporated into a program. This program is designed to read in a number representing the radius of a circle and to calculate the area of the circle using the formula (written in Pascal):

```
area := pi * radius * radius
```

We would normally write this formula as area $= 3.14$ x r^2, or something similar; the reason the formula looks like the above will be explained shortly.

```
program AreaOfCircle (input, output); {Program's name is AreaOfCircle}
{Data Declarations}
const
    pi = 3.14; {ConstantName is pi, value is 3.14}
var
    radius : real; {VariableName is radius, DataType is real}
    area   : real; {VariableName is area, DataType is real}
begin        {Main body of program}
    readln(radius);
    area := pi * radius * radius;
    writeln(area);
end.
```

The program is given the name, *AreaOfCircle*, because that is the function of the program; program names cannot include spaces (see below), so the name *Area of Circle* would not be allowed. There are two ways to get around this limitation and still keep program names, as well as variable and constant identifiers, meaningful. The first method is to use the approach above, that is, use a capital letter for the start of each word and place all of the words together without spaces; hence the identifier *AreaOfCircle*. The second method is to join the words together using underscores; this would produce the program identifier *area_of_circle* or *Area_of_Circle*. Both methods are popular. Many versions of Pascal allow the underscore to be used in identifiers; standard Pascal, however, does not and so the first method will be used from now on.

The rules that an identifier, or name, should adhere to are as follows:

(1)   An identifier should begin with a letter (upper or lower case).

(2)   The remainder of the identifier should contain only letters (upper or lower case) or digits or both.

(3)   An identifier should not be the same as any of Pascal's reserved words or special identifiers.

These are examples of correctly-formed identifiers:

    A,   A1,   Colin2,   Joe90,   abracadabra,   KilnPitRoad,   Q1234

and these are examples of incorrectly-formed identifiers:

    A 3,   6times,   Gerry!,   WhoAreYou?,   Bye-Bye,   begin

The constant *pi* is declared to be 3.14 and whenever *pi* is encountered in the main body of the program above it will be given that value. In some versions of Pascal *pi* will have been declared and given a value by the manufacturers (built in to the system, so to speak) and so the programmer will be able to refer to it in a program without having had first to declare it. Check your Pascal manual for details.

Two variables are required; one is used to store the value of the radius when it is read in from the keyboard (more about *readln* later) and one to hold the value of the area once it has been calculated by the formula. It makes sense to call these variables *radius* and *area* in order to make the program understandable but they could have just as easily been called *r* and *a*. However, these names are not nearly as meaningful as *radius* and *area*. It would have been perfectly acceptable to Pascal to have given these two variables names such as *Freddy1* and *Freddy2*. Obviously, these names bear no relation to the kind of data that they would be storing in the program and they would tend to confuse, and perhaps even annoy, another person trying to read and understand the program.

If the above program is compiled and then run it will first of all expect a number to be typed in; the *readln(radius)* statement will wait for the user to enter a number, representing the radius, and then expect the user to press *ENTER* to indicate that the input is complete. The program will output (using *writeln*, which will be discussed later) the value of the area in floating point form. For example, if the radius was given the value of 10 then the value of the area would appear on the monitor as 3.14E+02 or something similar; after all, the variable *area* was declared to be a real, which is just another way of saying that *area* will be stored as a floating point number. Writing numbers in the form of 3.14E+02 etc. is Pascal's way of saying 3.14×10^2 (i.e. 314.00), the *E* standing for *exponent* or *power of 10*. We will see later how to format the output of real numbers so that they will appear on the monitor as 314, 314.0, 314.00 etc.

The Assignment Operator

The previous program is repeated below:

```
program AreaOfCircle (input, output);
{Data Declarations}
const
     pi = 3.14;
var
     radius : real;
     area : real;
begin          {Main body of program}
     readln(radius);
     area : = pi * radius * radius;
     writeln(area);
end.
```

An *assignment statement* is one which gives or 'assigns' a value to a variable. In the program above, the statement:

area : = pi * radius * radius

is an assignment statement. The value of pi (3.14), multiplied by the radius and then multiplied by the radius again, is copied into the variable *area*. We say that *area* has been assigned a value. That value will obviously depend upon whatever value was contained in the variable *radius*. As mentioned earlier, if *radius* contained the value 10 then *area* would be assigned the value 314 (3.14 x 10 x 10). Remember, however, that it would be stored in floating point form.

The symbol ': =' is called the *assignment operator* and note that a space is not allowed between the ':' and the '=.' The symbol ': =' is called a compound symbol. The assignment operator must not be confused with the *equality operator* which is written as '='. Other examples of assignment statements are:

Xvalue : = 0; Sum : = FirstNumber + SecondNumber; y : = x * x;

FredsPay : = HarrysPay; YourFirst : = 6.12;

The format of an *assignment statement* is

VariableName : = **Expression;**

where **Expression**, in the case of integer or real variables, is any number (of the right data type) or arithmetic statement. It is possible to use integer variables and real variables in the same assignment statement; this will be discussed shortly.

Arithmetic Operators

Special symbols have to be used in arithmetic expressions; these are called the arithmetic operators and they are as follows:

for addition use	+
for subtraction use	−
for multiplication use	*
for division (of real numbers) use	/
for brackets use	()

Note that there is no Pascal arithmetic operator for raising a number to a power (or *exponent*) and so x^2 has to be written as x * x and y^3 has to be written as y * y * y and so on. There are some standard functions available for dealing with expressions involving exponents; these will be discussed in a later section.

It should now be starting to become clear why the formula for the area of a circle could not be written in Pascal as:

area = 3.14 x r^2

Integer Division

In the above list of arithmetic operators it should be noticed that the operator '/' is used for division of real numbers only. This is because Pascal is a *typed* language which means that the programmer must take care not to mix incompatible data types in an assignment statement (for details, see below). The problem with dividing one integer number by another integer number is that the result will not necessarily be an integer; the result may well contain a fractional part - in other words, the result will probably be a real! For example, 3 divided by 2 is 1.5.

Special operators are therefore provided for integer division; these are *div* and *mod*. *Div*, short for *divide*, gives the quotient or result of the division; *mod* gives the remainder or *modulus* after division. For example, *7 div 2* produces 3 (the quotient) and *7 mod 2* produces 1 (the remainder after division). These operators perform 'primary school' division, the type of division that we learned at school before we were aware of the existence of fractions and decimals.

Note that real numbers cannot use *div* and *mod*; for division of *real* numbers, only the operator '/' is allowed. It makes no sense trying to find the *mod* of two real numbers. A program illustrating the use of *div* and *mod* will be given shortly.

Data Type Compatibility

We can use different data types in the same arithmetic expression as long as we stick to Pascal's rules concerning *assignment compatibility*; that is, rules about which data types can be assigned to other data types. It is obvious that we can assign an integer value to an integer variable and a real value to a real variable. What may not be so obvious is that we are allowed to assign an integer value to a real variable but not a real value to an integer variable. An example should make this clear.

Suppose we have the following data declarations:

```
var
    Number1, Number2 : integer;
    Flop1, Flop2 : real;              {Flop is short for floating point or 'real'}
```

then the following *assignment* statements would be perfectly valid:

```
Flop1 := Number1 + Number2;   {Add two integers, place result in a real.}
Flop2 := 10;                  {Assign an integer value to a real variable.}
Flop1 := Flop2 + Number1;     {Add an integer to a real, place result in a real.}
Flop2 := Number1 div Number2; {Divide two integers, place result in a real.}
```

but the following assignment statements would be invalid:

```
Number1 := Flop1 + Flop2;     {Real result cannot be placed in an integer variable.}
Number2 := 3.9;               {Real value cannot be placed in an integer variable.}
Number1 := Number2 + Flop1;   {Real result cannot be placed in an integer variable.}
Number2 := Flop2;             {Cannot assign a real value to an integer variable.}
```

To summarize the above, we can write down two rules which state:

(1)   If integers and reals are used together in an expression, the resulting value will be a real. The result, therefore, must be assigned to a *real* variable.

(2)   Only integers are allowed to be mixed with integers if the result is to be assigned to an *integer* variable.

Arithmetic Operator Precedence

Each arithmetic operator has what is known as a *precedence* attached to it. The precedence of an operator determines its order of evaluation in an arithmetic statement. Programmers must be aware of this when writing programs containing arithmetic expressions. The higher the precedence of an operator the sooner it will be evaluated in any given expression. A precedence table of arithmetic operators is given below.

Operator	*Precedence*
()	highest (evaluated first)
* / div mod	
+ −	lowest (evaluated last)

Note that + and − have the same precedence and that *, /, div and mod have the same precedence.

To help explain the meaning of operator precedence consider the following expression:

```
5 + 6 * 2
```

Many people would say, incorrectly, that the result is 22; that is, 5 + 6 is 11, multiplying this by 2 gives 22. The actual result is 17 because multiplication (denoted by the operator *) has a higher precedence than addition (denoted by the operator +) and hence must be carried out first. So the 6 * 2 must be evaluated first, which comes to 12, and then adding the 5 to the 12 produces the result of 17.

If we wanted the result to be 22 then we would write the expression as:

(5 + 6) * 2

The brackets,(denoted by ()), have the highest precedence of all and this forces the 5 + 6 to be evaluated first.

If there are two or more operators of the same precedence, evaluation is carried out from left to right. For example:

3 + 6 – 2

gives a result of 7,

and

6 * 5 / 10

gives a result of 3.

The Readln Procedure

Assigning a value to a variable is one way of getting data into the computer's memory; for instance, if we wanted the variable *radius* to have the value 25, we could write

radius : = 25;

However, if this method is used, all the variables to be used in a program have to be given values before the program is run. If we wish to assign values to variables while the program is running then we need to use a *readln* statement; that is, a statement which uses Pascal's *readln* procedure. The *area* program given in the previous section used the statement

readln(radius);

to read in a value from the keyboard as the program was running.

A *readln* statement can be used with more than just one variable. For example, if we wished to read in a person's height and weight and store these values in the variables *height* and *weight* we could write

readln(height, weight);

If more than one data item is to be input using a single *readln* statement, each item must be entered with a space between it and the following item. For example, when inputting data using the statement

readln(height, weight);

we could type in *72 200* followed by pressing the *ENTER* key. The value 72 would be stored in the variable *height* and the value 200 would be stored in the variable *weight*. The space between them indicates that the two values are separate.

The format of the *readln* statement is:

readln(**variable1, variable2, variable3, etc.**);

and

readln;

Another example is

readln(day, month, year);

where the variables *day, month,* and *year* could have been declared as integers.

Typical data entered for this could be *4 8 56* (followed by pressing the *ENTER* key) which represents the 4th of August, 1956.

If *readln* is used on its own (without specifying a variable or variables) then it will accept anything we type in and wait for us to press the *ENTER* key; once we have hit *ENTER* the program will move on to the next statement. This can be used to our advantage. If we wish to temporarily halt a program, for example to output some results on the monitor and give the user time to read them before the program moves on, we can simply insert the statement *readln;* at the required point in the program. This will have the effect of stopping program execution until the *ENTER* key is pressed. Normally, we would precede the *readln* statement with a suitable message for the user, such as

Press the ENTER key when you are ready to continue.

This would be done using a *writeln* statement. (See next section).

The Writeln Procedure

The *writeln* procedure is used for outputting the values of variables and constants while a program is running and it has a format similar to the *readln* statement. The format is:

writeln(**variable1, variable2, etc., constant1, constant2, etc.**);

and

writeln;

Upon completion, a *writeln* statement places the cursor on a new line; this is the significance of the *ln* (short for line) at the end of the word *writeln.* Using *writeln* on its own has the effect of producing a blank line in the output. The statement

writeln;

simply writes nothing onto the current line and then places the cursor on the next line.

Notice that *writeln* can be used to output constants as well as variables; this makes the *writeln* statement very versatile. For example, the program to print out the message 'Hello, is there anyone out there?' used *writeln* to print out the message. This program is repeated below.

```
program simple (output);
begin
    writeln('Hello, is there anyone out there?');
end.
```

The message 'Hello, is there anyone out there?' is an example of a *string constant.* Note that string constants must be enclosed in single quotes and can contain whatever text is required (with the exception of the single quote! See below). The quotes do not appear in the output; they just tell Pascal that it is dealing with a string constant.

The *area* program in the last section used the statement

```
writeln(area);
```

to output onto the monitor the value of the area. The output could have also included the value of the radius that was input, that is,

```
writeln(radius, area);
```

but the output could be vastly improved by including some meaningful text so that it would read:

The radius and area are 1.0E+01 and 3.14E+02.

(Forget about the floating point numbers for the moment.)

The statement to do this is as follows

```
writeln('The radius and area are ', radius,' and ', area);
```

Note that the four items to be written out are separated by commas and that the list of outputted values consists of two variable values, that is, those contained in *radius* and *area*, and two string constants, that is, *'The radius and area are '* and *' and '*. Any text characters, including spaces, placed between the single quotes will be outputted, exactly as they are, to the monitor. Items without single quotes around them have to be variables or constants and the effect of the *writeln* statement on these is to output their contents onto the monitor.

The only problem character in a string constant is the single quote itself. For example, suppose the message, *The cat has eaten the dog's bone*, had to be written out. The quote in the word *dog's* would be mistaken as signalling the end of the message and the legitimate quote at the end of the string constant would be viewed by the compiler as an error because there would be three single quotes instead of two. The method here is to use two single quotes (with no spaces in between them) inside the message. This informs Pascal that the single quote is part of the contents of the string. The writeln statement would thus be:

```
writeln('The cat has eaten the dog''s bone');.
```

A further improvement to the area program could be in the form of a *prompt*. At the moment, when the program is run, it just 'sits there' waiting for the user to type in a value for the radius. The program would be more user friendly if it produced a message (or prompt) such as *Please enter a value for the radius*. This could be achieved very easily by including the statement:

```
writeln('Please enter a value for the radius');
```

The final improvement could be to *format* the output so that the user would not have to see the results written in floating point form. Formatting is carried out by adding special symbols to the variables or constants to be output. The output statement could now look like this:

```
writeln('The radius and area are ',radius:5:2,' and ',area:7:2);
```

This statement now has the effect of printing out *radius* in a field of 5 characters and with two decimal places and *area* in a field of seven characters also with two decimal places.

The *area* program is reproduced below with the improvements incorporated. The new version of the program is called *AreaOfCircle2*.

```
program AreaOfCircle2 (input, output);
{Data Declarations}
const
    pi = 3.14;
var
    radius : real;
    area : real;
begin        {Main body of program}
    writeln('Please input a value for the radius');
    readln(radius);
    area := pi * radius * radius;
    writeln('The radius and area are ',radius:5:2,' and ',area:7:2);
end.
```

To provide further illustration for formatting and also to show how to use *div* and *mod*, consider the program below.

```
program DivAndModEx (input, output);
var
    FirstNumber, SecondNumber, result1, result2 : integer;
begin
    writeln('Please type in two integer numbers');
    readln(Firstnumber, SecondNumber);
    result1 := FirstNumber div SecondNumber;
    result2 := FirstNumber mod SecondNumber;
    writeln;
    writeln('The results are as follows');
    writeln('result1 is ',result1:5,' result2 is ',result2:5);
end.
```

When this program is executed, the first output that appears is the prompt *Please type in two integer numbers*. The user must then type in the two numbers, on the same line and leaving a space between them, and then press the *enter* key to complete the data entry. The variables *result1* and *result2* will then be assigned the appropriate values. A blank line will be 'printed' (achieved by using *writeln* without an output list) followed by the string *The results are as follows* on the next line. The final line will then be printed and will be of the form:

        result1 is   22   result2 is   3

Note that integer variables, like real variables, can be formatted for output. Unlike real variables, however, there is no reason to supply the number of places after the decimal point because integers don't need decimal points! In this program the values of the variables *result1* and *result2* will each be outputted in a field of five characters; hence the spaces before the *22* and the *3*. Note that when formatting is used, items are right-justified (that is, placed at the right hand side) within the specified field width.

Returning to the *readln* statement in the above program; if preferred, two separate *readln* statements could have been used instead of one, as follows:

```
readln(FirstNumber);
readln(SecondNumber);
```

In this case, the user would have to type in the value of each variable on a separate line by pressing the *ENTER* key after each value.

The Write Procedure

There are times when we might want to output a message to the user and prefer that the cursor remain on the same line as the message; remember that *writeln* will place the cursor on a new line after it has finished its output. The way to do this is to use the *write* procedure which will place the cursor at the position following the last character to be output.

A *write* statement is preferrable to a *writeln* statement when prompting the user to input some data. It certainly looks better if the cursor is flashing at the end of the message rather than on the next line. The statements needed to output the message *Please input the price* and read in the price would be as shown below:

```
write('Please input the price ');
readln(Price);.
```

Note the space after the word *price* so that the cursor is not flashing directly after it.

Write statements have the same format as *writeln* statements.

Successive *write* statements will simply write data onto the current line; of course, when the end of the current line is reached, output will be forced onto the next line. You may wonder if there is a matching *read* statement; there is, but a discussion of the *read* procedure will be left to a later section in the book.

Practice Programs

The following programs are intended to be keyed in and executed. The idea is to help you get used to Pascal, by becoming familiar with Pascal's special words and punctuation.

(a)

```
program SumAndDiff (input, output);
{program to find the sum and difference of two numbers}
var
      number1, number2 : integer;
      sum, difference : integer;
begin
      readln(number1);
      readln(number2);
      sum := number1 + number2;
      difference := number1 - number2;
      writeln(sum,' ', difference);
end.
```

(b)

```
program CalculateVat (input, output);
{program to calculate the VAT (Value Added Tax) on a sales item}
const
     VatRate = 0.15;
var
     cost, vat, BillTotal : real;
begin
     readln(cost);
     vat : = cost * VatRate;
     BillTotal : = cost + vat;
     writeln(cost:6:2);
     writeln(vat:6:2);
     writeln(BillTotal:6:2);
end.
```

(c)

```
program Rectangle (input, output);
{program to calculate the area and perimeter of a rectangle}
var
     length, breadth, area, perimeter : real;
begin
     readln(length, breadth);
     area : = length * breadth;
     perimeter : = 2 * (length + breadth);
     writeln('area is ',area:7:3,' perimeter is ',perimeter:5:3);
end.
```

Exercises

1   Rewrite programs (a), (b) and (c) so that they are more user friendly; that is, supply *prompts* for the user and improve the look of the output.

2   Write a program to read in five numbers and calculate the total and average of the five numbers.
(To get the average, just divide the total by 5.)

3   Write a program to read in a value (using a *real* variable) representing an amount in pounds sterling, and which writes out the equivalent value in dollars, francs, lire and marks.
N.B. You may need to look up the current exchange rates for these currencies.

4 Write a program to carry out these tasks:

  (i) Read in a whole number (integer) representing an amount in pounds.

  (ii) Divide this amount by 7

  (iii) Output the result along with any remainder. Note: Decimal fractions are not allowed in this program so you must use *div* and *mod*.

5 Use *div* and *mod* in a program to read in an integer representing a number of seconds and which outputs the corresponding value in hours, minutes and seconds. For example, if 3661 is entered, the result should be 1 hour, 1 minute and 1 second. (60 seconds = 1 minute, 3600 seconds = 1 hour.)

6 Write a program to read three numbers into the integer variables *I, J* and *K,* and to produce output in the format given below:

$$I =$$
$$J =$$
$$K =$$
$$I + J =$$
$$J - K =$$
$$J * K =$$
$$I \text{ div } J =$$
$$I \text{ mod } J =$$

7 Evaluate the following expressions (don't forget precedence).

  (i) 2 + 3 * 3 + 4

  (ii) 7 - 6 / 3

  (iii) 15 mod 4 - 2

  (iv) 4 * (4 / 2 + 6 / 2) / 2

  (v) 9 * 3 div 4

Chapter 2

Control Statements

Loop Control

The idea of a *loop* is fundamental to programming. A loop is required whenever the same operations are to be repeated over and over again, each time using different items of data. For example, a table of the square roots of a set of numbers may be required. Here, each number will be subjected to the same operation (that is, finding the root) in order to produce the table. A second example is that of invoicing in a data processing department. Each invoice will be treated identically by the computer; at a simple level the operations could consist of looking up the price of each item, adding that price to the running total, and then calculating the VAT.

It should be obvious that without loops, programs would become vast sequences of identical operations requiring large computer memories for their storage. In addition, computer programs would take much longer to write.

Pascal offers the programmer three types of loop: the *for..to..do* loop, the *repeat..until* loop and the *while..do* loop. These will now be discussed in turn, each one being used to produce a program which calculates the average of a set of numbers.

The For..To..Do Loop

This form of loop is normally used when the programmer knows in advance how many times the loop will be traversed. The program below is designed to calculate the average of 10 numbers. The numbers will be input by the user at run time.

```
program AverageNo1 (input, output);
var
        number, total, average : real;
        count : integer;
begin
        total : = 0;
        for count : = 1 to 10 do
            begin
                readln(number);
                total : = total + number;
            end;
        average : = total / 10;
        writeln('The average is ',average:8:2);
    end.
```

Points to note about this program are:

(1) The variable *count* is declared as an integer. This variable is used as the *loop control variable*; it keeps track of the number of times that the for..to..do loop has been executed. It *must* be declared as an integer because a loop can only be executed an integral number of times; it is impossible, and would indeed be undesirable, to execute a loop 3.8 times, for example. As with all variables, loop control variables should be given names (identifiers) appropriate to the task being carried out.

(2) The statement

```
for count : = 1 to 10 do
```

can be read as 'for the value of count running from 1 up to 10 (in steps of 1) do whatever follows', or more simply as, 'execute the following statements 10 times'. The statements to be carried out over and over again are listed between the words *begin* and *end* which follow the *do* statement. These statements form what is known as a *block*. In this case, the block of statements to be carried out 10 times consists of the statements *readln(number);* and
total := total + number;.

If only one statement is to be carried out in the loop, the words *begin* and *end* can be omitted; for example as in

```
for count : = 1 to 100 do
      writeln(count);
```

which will display the numbers 1 to 100 on the monitor. Notice that here, the loop control variable is also being used to produce the necessary values to be output. This is a common programming technique.

(3) The value of *total* is initialized to 0 before the loop begins. It is wise to always initialize variables representing running totals, counts etc., because variables can sometimes retain values from previous program executions. Try taking out the statement

```
total : = 0;
```

and then running the program a few times. Does the program get the average right each time? See how your computer copes. It may reset all variables before each program execution, but then again it may not. My computer certainly does not!

(4) The statement

```
total : = total + number
```

may look rather odd to you. In terms of algebra this appears to be an impossible statement; how can *total* be equal to *total* + *number*? It must be remembered that the symbol *:=* does not mean 'equal to', it is actually the assignment operator. This statement should be read as 'the new value of *total* becomes equal to the old value of *total* with the value of *number* added to it'. In other words, *number* is added to *total* to produce a new value in *total*. This is an example of a running total; each time a number is input it is added to the current value in total.

(5) The average is computed by simply dividing total by 10.

The program above could easily be made more flexible by allowing any number of numbers to be input rather than just 10 every time. This could be done by asking the user, at the beginning of the program, to specify the number of numbers to be averaged. A new variable *amount* could be used to hold this value.

The program now looks as follows:

```
program AverageNo2 (input, output);
var
      number, total, average : real;
      count, amount : integer;
begin
      total : = 0;
      writeln('How many numbers will you be entering?');
      readln(amount);
      for count : = 1 to amount do
          begin
              readln(number);
              total : = total + number;
          end;
      average : = total / amount;
      writeln('The average is ',average:8:2);
end.
```

The loop will now be executed as many times as specified in *amount* and the average will now be calculated by dividing the total by *amount*.

Sometimes it is necessary to have the loop control variable count backwards; instead of going 1, 2, 3, ... to 10, for example, we may like to have the sequence go 10, 9, 8, 7, ... down to 1. This is accomplished by using the reserved word *downto* instead of *to*. The program below writes out the numbers from 20 down to 5 in order.

```
program DownCount (input, output);
var
      number : integer;
begin
      for number : = 20 downto 5 do
          writeln(number);
end.
```

To summarize, the format of the *for..to..do* is

      for **LoopControlVariable** : = **StartingValue** to **FinishingValue** do **Statement**

or

      for **LoopControlVariable** : = **StartingValue** to **FinishingValue** do
          begin
              Statement Block
          end

or

      for **LoopControlVariable** : = **StartingValue** downto **FinishingValue** do **Statement**

or

      for **LoopControlVariable** : = **StartingValue** downto **FinishingValue** do
         begin
            Statement Block
         end

The Repeat..Until Loop

This form of loop is used in any situation where repetitive operations are to be carried out *until* some particular condition becomes *true*. The program below uses a *repeat..until* loop to find the average of 12 numbers; once again, the numbers are to be input at run time.

```
program AverageNo3 (input, output);
var
      number, total, average : real;
      count : integer;
begin
      total : = 0;
      count : = 0;                          {Set the count and the total to zero.}
         repeat
            readln(number);
            total : = total + number;       {Add number read in to running total.}
            count : = count + 1;            {Add 1 to the count.}
         until count = 12;
      average : = total / 12;
      writeln('The average is ',average:8:2);
end.
```

The reserved words *repeat* and *until* form the boundary of the loop. The block of statements inside the loop will be executed over and over again until the *condition* for ending the loop becomes true. The condition for terminating the loop is *count = 12*. As each number is input the count is increased (or *incremented*) by 1. This is carried out by using the variable *count*; each time the loop is executed, 1 is added to the value of *count* using the statement *count := count + 1*. Each time the end of the loop is encountered, that is, the word *until* is reached, the question *is count = 12?* is posed. If the count is not equal to 12 then the loop is executed again; this continues until a count of 12 is reached, at which point the loop *condition* is *true* and the loop is exited. Finally, the average is calculated and the result written to the monitor.

The format of the *repeat..until* loop is

    repeat
        statements
    until **condition**

The While..Do Loop

It would be nice if the previous averaging program could be re-written so that the user could type in numbers without having to specify in advance how many numbers to expect. (The user may not know in advance how many numbers will be input.) Termination of the loop in this type of situation requires that some special signal be given to the program to inform it that the user has no more numbers to input.

One way of doing this is to input a *sentinel* or *rogue* value to the running program to inform it that data entry is complete. A rogue value is a piece of data having a certain value which will be used as a trigger to halt the loop. Rogue values should be chosen carefully; if a piece of valid data has the same value as the rogue then it will inadvertently terminate the program. The following program is *an attempt* to accept any number of positive values and then to calculate the average of those values. The rogue value is chosen to be –999; to terminate the loop and hence allow the program to finish, the user must type in the value –999 once all the valid items of data have been entered.

```
program AverageNo4 (input, output);
{Beware, this program contains a bug!}
var
      number, total, average : real;
      count : integer;
begin
      total : = 0;
      count : = 0;
         repeat
             readln(number);
             total : = total + number;
             count : = count + 1;
          until number = –999;
      average : = total / count;
      writeln('The average is ',average:8:2);
 end.
```

This program runs smoothly but it produces incorrect output. The problem is, we have added the rogue value to the running total and to make matters worse, we have added an extra 1 to our count of numbers that were input; that is, we have included the rogue in our number count. Ideally, we should check each number as it is, input to see if it is the rogue value; if it is, then the loop should be exited immediately; if it is not the rogue value, then the count should be incremented and the number added to the running total. The next program, called AverageNo5, does this correctly by using a *while..do* loop.

```
program AverageNo5 (input, output);
var
        number, total, average : real;
        count : integer;
begin
        total : = 0;
        count : = 0;
        readln(number);
        while number < > –999 do    {Execute loop if number is not equal to the rogue}
            begin
                total : = total + number;
                count : = count + 1;
                readln(number);
            end;
        average : = total / count;        {Calculate the average.}
        writeln('The average is ',average:8:2);
    end.
```

The difference between a *while..do* and a *repeat..until* loop is simply that a *while..do* tests the condition *before* the loop is traversed but a *repeat..until* tests the condition *after* the loop is traversed. This means that with a *repeat..until* loop the statements in the loop must be executed at least once; the statements in a *while..do* loop may, if necessary, not be executed at all.

The *condition* following the word *while* is tested, and if it is found to be *true*, the body of the loop is executed. The body of the loop could be just one statement or a block of statements. Should the latter be the case, then the statements must be enclosed between the words *begin* and *end*. (As in the case of a *for..to..do* statement.)

Note that in program AverageNo5 it is necessary to have a *readln(number)* statement before the loop is entered. If the condition *number < > –999* (which means *is number not equal to –999?*) is true then the body of the loop is executed. The last statement inside the loop is *readln(number)* and this is required at this point so that when control returns back to the statement *while number < >–999*, a decision can be made about whether to execute the loop again or else exit the loop and continue with the next statement. In the latter case the next statement is the one which calculates the average.

The format of the *while..do* loop is

```
while condition do statement
```

or

```
while condition do
    begin
        statements
    end
```

Loop Conditions

At this stage it is necessary to look at the format of loop conditions. Firstly, we need to know which *relational operators* are allowed. We have already met some in the programs above. A table of relational operators is shown below:

Operator	Meaning
=	is equal to
< >	is not equal to
>	is greater than
<	is less than
> =	is greater than or equal to
< =	is less than or equal to

The most basic format of a *condition* is:

VariableName1   **relational operator**   **VariableName2**

or

VariableName   **relational operator**   **ConstantName**

Some examples are:

rate1 > rate2,   x = y,   x > 36,   total > 100,   result < > 0,   RateOfPay > = 3.75, MyHeight < = YourHeight

More complex forms of conditions will be discussed later.

Conditions are used in situations other than in loop control; the *if..then..else* statement, which will be described shortly, also requires the inclusion of some form of condition.

Nesting of Loops

A loop can be placed inside another loop, which in turn can be placed inside another loop and so on. When loops are used in this way they are said to be *nested*. The depth of nesting, that is, how many loops are placed inside other loops, can be carried out to any level required. Normally, however, a depth of three of four is about the maximum required by most programs. The next program, called NestedLoop, demonstrates how one *for..to..do* loop can be nested inside another *for..to..do* loop.

```
program NestedLoop (output);
var
     x : integer;
     y : integer;
     sum : integer;
     product : integer;
begin
     for x : = 1 to 4 do
         for y : = 1 to 5 do
             begin
                 sum : = x + y;
                 product : = x * y;
                 writeln('x =',x,' y =',y,' sum =',sum,' product =',product);
             end;
end.
```

The outer loop, controlled by the variable x is executed 4 times; for each of these 4 repetitions the inner loop, controlled by the variable y, is executed 5 times. Thus, the inner loop is executed 20 (4 x 5) times, each repetition causing the sum and product of x and y to be calculated and printed out, along with the x and y values.

Another nested loop is shown below in the program called Delay, which does just that. The program executes the inner loop 1 million times (1000 x 1000) doing absolutely nothing except creating a time delay. The length of the delay will depend upon the processor speed of your computer. Experiment with the program by increasing or decreasing the number of loop traversals, e.g. try x = 2000, y = 3000 and try to produce delays of exactly 1, 2, and 3 seconds. For really long delays you could place a third (z) loop inside the y loop. Don't go overboard though - you could wait a long time for the program to finish!

```
program Delay;                         {Requires no input or output.}
var
     x : integer;
     y : integer;
begin
     for x : = 1 to 1000 do
         for y : = 1 to 1000 do;        {Do nothing a million times!}
end.
```

It may be worth checking the version of Pascal you are using to see if it contains a built-in function to produce a delay of a certain length. Some versions have a routine that is actually called *delay* and which you call up with the number of milliseconds (that is, thousandths of a second) that you require the delay to last. For example, by including the statement

```
delay(2000);
```

a delay of 2 seconds will be produced at that position in your program. Delays are useful in situations where you require messages etc. to remain on-screen for a pre-determined time before they disappear. An as example, suppose you were writing a quiz program which gave a candidate 5 seconds to read each question before the question disappeared from the monitor; you could write statements such as the following:

```
writeln('You have 5 seconds to read this question');
writeln;
writeln('What is the capital of Denmark?');
delay(5000); {Hold the screen for 5 seconds.}
{Clear the screen here. See if your version of Pascal contains}
{a special routine (e.g. clrscr) to do this.}
```

The If..Then..Else Statement

Computers can be programmed to make simple decisions such as 'is 5 greater than 6?' and 'is x equal to y?'. Without the ability to make decisions like these, computers would be relatively useless; they would simply be calculators. It is the inclusion of a logical decision-making unit that distinguishes a computer from a calculator. In Pascal, the *if..then..else* statement is used when we wish to program a decision. A shortened version of the *if..then..else* can be used, where appropriate; this is the *if..then* statement.

The basic format of the *if..then..else* statement is:

if **condition** then **statement1** else **statement2**

In English this can be read as follows:

'If the condition is true then carry out statement1 or else (that is, if the condition is not true) carry out statement2.'

Conditions are written in the manner described earlier - see the section on loops. As an illustration, the following program, called decision1, reads in a number from the keyboard and then checks (or decides) whether the number is zero or not. Note that there is no semi-colon inside the *if..then..else* statement; newcomers to Pascal often insert semi-colons into these statements at places where they are not required - especially at the end of the line before the word *else*. Remember that a semi-colon signals the end of a Pascal statement; should the word *else* follow straight after a semi-colon, it means that the word *else* must be at the start of a new statement. This is, of course, a grammatical error or *syntax error* because there is no Pascal statement that begins with the word *else*.

```
program decision1 (input, output);
var
    number : real;
begin
    writeln('Please enter a number');
    readln(number);
    if number = 0 then       {Perform statement1}
        writeln('The number you have entered is zero')
    else      {Perform statement2}
        writeln('The number you have entered is not zero');
end.
```

The decision to be made here is whether or not the variable *number* is equal to zero, so the condition is *number = 0*? If *number* is equal to zero (that is, *number = 0* is true) then the statement *writeln('The number you have entered is zero')* is carried out. If *number* is not equal to zero (that is, *number = 0* is false) then the statement *writeln('The number you have entered is not zero')* is carried out.

Carrying this a stage further, suppose that now we are interested in whether the number to be inputted is zero, positive or negative; this requires two decisions to be made:

    (1) Is the number 0?

    (2) If it isn't 0, is it positive or negative?

The programming for this is shown below in program decision2.

```
program decision2 (input, output);
var
     number : real;
begin
     writeln('Please enter a number');
     readln(number);
     if number = 0 then
          writeln('The number you have entered is zero')
     else
          if number < 0 then
               writeln('The number you have entered is negative')
          else
               writeln('The number you have entered is positive');
end.
```

The condition *number = 0* is used to decide whether or not *number* contains a zero. If it does then the statement *writeln('The number you have entered is zero')* is carried out. If *number* does not contain zero then another *if..then..else* statement is carried out. This uses the condition *number < 0* to decide if the number is positive or negative. Note that at this point in the program, the value stored in the variable called *number* cannot possibly be equal to zero.

This program demonstrates the idea of nested *if..then..else* statements; one *if..then..else* statement is placed inside another *if..then..else* statement. Nesting of *if..then..else* statements can be carried out to any depth required. Unfortunately, when many *if..then..else* statements are nested, the logic of the statements can become difficult to understand and result in incorrect program action. Exercise number 5 at the end of the chapter illustrates this. This exercise should not be attempted, however, until the section on character variables has been read.

Often we require more than one statement to be carried out following the decision. This is accomplished by placing the block of statements to be carried out between the words *begin* and *end*, in the manner used in the *for..to..do* loop. On the next page you will find a program, decision3, which demonstrates this.

```
program decision3 (input, output);
var
     number : real;
begin
     writeln('Please enter a number');
     readln(number);
     if number = 0 then
          writeln('The number you have entered is zero')
     else
          if number < 0 then   {Perform first block of statements}
               begin
                    writeln('The number you have entered is negative');
                    writeln('Its value was ',number:12:2);
               end
          else {Perform second block of statements}
               begin
                    writeln('The number you have entered is positive');
                    writeln('Its value was ',number:12:2);
               end;
end.
```

In the above program, if the number is positive or negative then the value of the number is written out along with the message declaring it to be positive or negative.

This additional *if..then..else* format can be written as

```
if condition then
     begin
          statement block1
     end
else
     begin
          statement block2
     end
```

As mentioned earlier, the *else* part of the *if..then..else* statement can be omitted if required; for example, in a situation where we are testing to see if something is true and we are not interested if that something is not true. Consider the situation where we have a set of numbers and if any of the numbers are found to be negative, then they have to be made positive; –6, for example, will become +6 (or just 6).

The program, decision4, on the next page illustrates this.

```
program decision4 (input, output);
var
      number : real;
      x : integer;
begin
      for x : = 1 to 10 do
            begin
                  readln(number);
                  if number < 0 then
                        number : = number * −1;
                  writeln(number:12:2);
            end;
end.
```

After the *readln(number)* statement is executed, an *if..then* statement is used to check whether or not the current number is less than 0. If it is less than zero then the number is multiplied by -1 to make it positive; if it is already positive (or zero) then no action need be taken. Hence, the *else* part of the statement is not required.

The format is thus: if **condition** then **statement**

Compound Conditions

Sometimes a decision requires more than one condition; this is a situation where a *compound condition* is needed. A compound condition consists of ordinary (or simple) conditions joined together by the reserved words *or* and *and*, which are known as *boolean operators*. Furthermore, each separate condition is placed in round brackets.

Suppose we have a situation where we are comparing three numbers which are stored in the variables *number1*, *number2* and *number3* and we would like to print out *number2* if it is greater than *number1* and also greater than *number3*. The statement to do this is as follows:

```
if (number2 > number1) and (number2 > number3) then
      writeln(number2);
```

Should we wish to print out *number2* if it is greater than *number1* or *number3*, that is, it need only be greater than one of them, then the statement would become:

```
if (number2 > number1) or (number2 > number3) then
      writeln(number2);
```

The above examples illustrate situations where the compound condition consists of two simple conditions but if need be a compound condition can consist of as many simple conditions as is required. The statement fragment below shows this:

```
if (x = 0) or (x = 1) or (x = 3) or (x = 2) and (y = 0) then
      {do whatever is required at this point}
```

One point to note about this statement is that the compound condition consists of 3 simple conditions,

$(x = 0)$, $(x = 1)$ and $(x = 3)$,

which are all 'or'ed together (connected with or's) and a fourth condition

$(x = 2)$ and $(y = 0)$,

which is itself a compound condition.

This latter condition may look like two simple conditions but the inclusion of the *and* operator means that both of the conditions $(x = 2)$ and $(y = 0)$ have to be true for this latter compound condition to evaluate to true. The reason for the $(x = 2)$ and the $(y = 0)$ conditions being 'tied closely together', so to speak, is that boolean operators (*and, or* etc.) have precedences in the same way that the arithmetic operators have precedences. The operator *and* has a higher precedence than the operator *or* and so the $(x = 2)$ condition must be 'and'ed with the $(y = 0)$ condition first. This compound condition is then considered to be 'or'ed with the other conditions $(x = 0)$, $(x = 1)$ and $(x = 3)$.

So the four conditions, each of which can make the overall condition be equal to true are as follows:

$(x = 0)$, $(x = 1)$, $(x = 3)$, and $(x = 2)$ and $(y = 0)$.

The original statement could be made more explicit by adding an extra set of brackets around the fourth condition so that it becomes:

if $(x = 0)$ or $(x = 1)$ or $(x = 3)$ or $((x = 2)$ and $(y = 0))$ then

{do whatever is required at this point}.

It can be seen that the extra brackets emphasise the fact that the last condition is a compound one.

Apart from *and* and *or* there is a boolean operator called *not*. The effect of *not* is to invert the meaning of a statement or condition. For example, if we wished to write a program fragment which would print out the message 'Hello, hello' if both of the conditions $(x = 1)$ and $(y = 2)$ were *not* true then we could write:

if not $((x = 1)$ and $(y = 2))$ then

write('Hello, hello');.

The extra pair of brackets around the two conditions *are* necessary in this case because the *not* operator has the highest precedence of all the boolean operators; writing the statement in the form

if not $(x = 1)$ and $(y = 2)$ then

write('Hello, hello');

would cause the condition to be true if $(x = 1)$ was not true (the *not* is now only applied to the first condition because it has a higher precedence than the *and*) and $(y = 2)$ was true. This clearly makes a difference to the meaning of the condition. Note that, whereas the operators *and* and *or* operate on pairs of conditions, the *not* operator operates on only one condition. *And* and *or* are called *binary operators* (like add and subtract) but *not* is a *unary operator* (it behaves in the way that the minus sign - the unary minus - does in the expression $(-3 * X)$).

To summarise then, the precedence table for the boolean operators is as follows:

Operator	Precedence
not	highest (evaluated first)
and	
or	lowest (evaluated last)

Truth Tables

Any condition or expression which can be evaluated as being *true* or *false* is known as a *boolean expression*. So the conditions (or expressions)

(a) X < = 23   (b) (X + Y) = 30   (c) not (Fred > Harry)

(d) (You – Me) or (Him + Her)   (e) (C = 3 + D) and (E < 5)

are all boolean expressions because, depending upon the values of the variables used in the expressions, they are all either *true* or *false*; we say they evaluate to either *true* or *false*. *Truth tables* can be drawn up which show how the truth value of an expression is evaluated by a computer.

Considering example (e) we say that this expression consists of two *operands* which are *(C = 3 + D)* and *(E < 5)*. We can thus refer to these operands as operand1 and operand2. *Operands* are simply the entities (or things) that *operators* operate on. In example (e) then, for the whole expression to be true, both of the operands, operand1 and operand2, have to be true because they are connected together (that is, '*and*'ed together) by the *and* operator.

The *truth tables* below show how the operators *and, or* and *not* evaluate the results of boolean expressions:

The **AND** operator

operand1	operand2	result (operand1 *and* operand2)
true	true	true
true	false	false
false	true	false
false	false	false

The **OR** operator

operand1	operand2	result (operand1 or operand2)
true	true	true
true	false	true
false	true	true
false	false	false

The **NOT** operator

operand	result (not operand)
true	false
false	true

The Case Statement

Sometimes, whole sequences of repetitive-looking *if..then* statements are required. For example, suppose we require a program which accepts a number, in the range 1 to 12, which represents a month; month 1 is January, month 2 is February and so on and we wish to compute the number of days in that month (ignoring leap years for the sake of clarity). One possible solution might be to write the following, where *month* and *NoOfDays* have been declared as integer variables:

```
if month = 1  then NoOfDays : = 31;
if month = 2  then NoOfDays : = 28;
if month = 3  then NoOfDays : = 31;
if month = 4  then NoOfDays : = 30;
if month = 5  then NoOfDays : = 31;
if month = 6  then NoOfDays : = 30;
if month = 7  then NoOfDays : = 31;
if month = 8  then NoOfDays : = 31;
if month = 9  then NoOfDays : = 30;
if month = 10 then NoOfDays : = 31;
if month = 11 then NoOfDays : = 30;
if month = 12 then NoOfDays : = 31;.
```

The result looks less than appealing. Of course, we could reduce the number of statements by using compound conditions such as:

```
if (month = 4) or (month = 6) or (month = 9) or (month = 11) then
    NoOfDays : = 30;
```

but there is, however, a much neater way to do this by using the *case* statement. The *case* statement allows the above statements to be rewritten as shown on the next page:

```
case month of
     1 : NoOfDays := 31;
     2 : NoOfDays := 28;
     3 : NoOfDays := 31;
     4 : NoOfDays := 30;
     5 : NoOfDays := 31;
     6 : NoOfDays := 30;
     7 : NoOfDays := 31;
     8 : NoOfDays := 31;
     9 : NoOfDays := 30;
     10: NoOfDays := 31;
     11: NoOfDays := 30;
     12: NoOfDays := 31;
end;
```

which looks better and is easier to read; the statement is read as 'in the case of (the variable) *month* being equal to 1, set the number of days (variable *NoOfDays*) to 31, etc.'. We can go one better and simply group together the values of month that refer to 28, 30 and 31 days as follows:

```
case month of
     1, 3, 5, 7, 8, 10, 12      : NoOfDays := 31;
     4, 6, 9, 11                : NoOfDays := 30;
     2                          : NoOfDays := 28;
end;
```

Most versions of Pascal have extended the *case* statement so that an *else* (or *otherwise* in some versions) can be included; this can be used to trap incorrect data. For example, if a user typed in 13 then this would have to be dealt with in some way because there is no month 13. The next program, CaseDemo, illustrates this.

```
program CaseDemo (input, output);
var
     NoOfDays, month : integer;
begin
     write('Enter a month between 1 and 12 ');
     readln(month);
     case month of
          1, 3, 5, 7, 8, 10, 12 : NoOfDays := 31;
          4, 6, 9, 11           : NoOfDays := 30;
          2                     : NoOfDays := 28;
          else NoOfDays := 0; {Trap incorrect entry}
     end;
     if NoOfDays = 0 then
          writeln('Incorrect Data Entered')
     else
          writeln('Month number ',month,' has ',NoOfDays,' days');
end.
```

If the entered value of *month* is outside of the range 1 to 12 then the *else* part of the statement sets the value of *NoOfDays* to 0. The *if..then..else* statement following the *case* statement uses the condition *NoOfDays = 0* to output an error message to the user.

The basic format of the *case* statement is

```
case VariableName of
     Value1 : Statement1;
     Value2 : Statement2;
     etc.
     ValueN : StatementN
end
```

As with the other Pascal constructs (*if..then..else* etc.), should more than one statement be required for any particular value, then these statements must be enclosed between the words *begin* and *end*.

To summarize, the *case* statement is useful when one of several alternatives need to be selected, and is especially useful when the selection is to be based on the value of a single variable. The *case* statement, however, cannot be used with some types of variables, notably reals. Strictly speaking, the *case* statement can only be used with variables of *ordinal type*, such as integers. Ordinal types will be discussed in detail later.

Character Variables

So far, only the variable types *integer* and *real* have been discussed. It is time to introduce a new type of variable called *char*, which is short for *character*. A variable of this type can hold just one character. The character stored can be any character in the ASCII code set (see appendix for details), for example, 'a', 'A', '@', '+', and non-printable characters such as carriage return (CR), line feed (LF) and escape (ESC). If the computer you are using recognises other characters as well, such as extended key code characters, then they can also be stored in character variables.

Character variables can be assigned values in the same manner as integer and real variables. For instance, to assign the value *Y* to a character variable called *reply*, we would write:

```
reply : = 'Y';.
```

Note that single quotes are required around the character. In a condition, we might write something such as

```
reply < > 'n' (that is, reply not equal to 'n')
```

To illustrate the use of a *char* variable in a program, a program from the section on loops will be used (program AverageNo3) and altered accordingly. The program, prior to amendment, is shown below.

```
program AverageNo3 (input, output);
var
      number, total, average : real;
      count : integer;
begin
      total : = 0;
      count : = 0;
          repeat
              readln(number);
              total : = total + number;
              count : = count + 1;
          until count = 12;
      average : = total / 12;
      writeln('The average is ',average:8:2);
end.
```

At the moment this program can only deal with 12 numbers being input; the program will be
altered so that after each number is input, the user will be asked if there are any more numbers
to be input. If there are, the program will continue; if not the program will calculate the
average and then stop. The user's reply to the question *'Are there any more numbers to be
input?'* will be stored in a character variable called *reply* and will be used in the condition for
terminating the *repeat..until* loop. The user is expected to type in either 'y' or 'n'. The
amended program is shown below and is now called AverageNo6.

```
program AverageNo6 (input, output);
var
      number, total, average : real;
      count : integer;
      reply : char;{reply is declared to be a character variable}
begin
      total : = 0;
      count : = 0;
          repeat
              readln(number);
              total : = total + number;
              count : = count + 1;
              writeln('Are there any more numbers to be input (y/n)?');
              readln(reply);
          until reply = 'n';
      average : = total / count;
      writeln('The average is ',average:8:2);
end.
```

If you run this program you will find that you actually do not need to type 'y' to continue with
the program; any old symbol will do, except 'n' of course, because the condition for

terminating the loop is simply that *reply* has to be equal to 'n'. Also, it doesn't matter if you type in 'yes' or 'yesterday' for 'y' and 'no' or 'nobody' for 'n'! A character variable will only take the first character that is read and ignore the others.

The program does have a drawback, though, and that is the fact that it will not terminate if 'N' (uppercase of 'n') is typed in. The remedy for this is to simply rewrite the loop terminating statement as

```
until (reply = 'n') or (reply = 'N');
```

which uses a compound condition; now either 'n' or 'N' will terminate the loop. If the version of Pascal you are using contains a function which will convert a lower case character to its upper case form (such as *upcase* in Turbo Pascal) then a neater solution would be to rewrite the *until* statement as

```
until upcase(reply) = 'N';
```

which literally means 'until the upper case value of *reply* is equal to 'N''.

As a further example, the program below (CheckLetters), asks the user for 12 letters, one at a time, and then informs the user of the number of vowels and the number of consonants typed in.

```
program CheckLetters (input, output);
var
    x, ConsonantCount, VowelCount : integer;
    letter : char;
begin
    ConsonantCount : = 0; {Initialize counting variables}
    VowelCount : = 0;
    for x : = 1 to 12 do
        begin
            writeln('Please type in a letter');
            readln(letter);
            if (letter = 'a') or (letter = 'e') or (letter = 'i') or (letter = 'o') or
            (letter = 'u') then
                VowelCount : = VowelCount + 1
            else ConsonantCount : = ConsonantCount + 1;
        end;
    writeln('Number of vowels:',VowelCount);
    writeln('Number of consonants:',ConsonantCount);
end.
```

Note how the *if..then..else* statement is used. There is a compound condition (of 'or'ed simple conditions) to check for vowels (that is, the letters 'a', 'e', 'i', 'o' and 'u'). If one of these letters is detected then the variable *VowelCount* is incremented by 1; if not then the variable *ConsonantCount* is incremented by 1. There is no need to actually check for consonants since the *else* takes care of them.

Characters can be compared with each other. For example, the character 'b' is considered to be greater than the character 'a'. One way to look at this is to consider that 'b' is further down the alphabet than 'a' is; computers consider that 'b' is greater than 'a' because the ASCII code for 'b', which is 98, is greater than the ASCII code for 'a' which is 97. Thus characters, and hence whole words, can easily be sorted alphabetically by computer. Comparisons are made using the same *relational operators* as are used for numerical comparisons, that is, the operators =, < >, >, <, > = and < = .

The program below, called CapsCheck, shows how to check whether an input character is uppercase or not. The variable, *letter*, is checked to see if it holds a character which lies between 'A' and 'Z'. This is accomplished by using the relational operators > = and < =.

```
program CapsCheck (input, output);
var
     letter : char;
begin
     writeln('Enter a capital letter');
     readln(letter);
     if (letter > = 'A') and (letter < = 'Z')  then
          writeln('You did enter a capital letter')
     else
          writeln('You did not enter a capital letter - naughty!');
end.
```

Finally, the program below, CharCompare, shows how two characters can be compared and then written out in correct alphabetic order.

```
program CharCompare (input, output);
var
     letter1, letter2 : char;
begin
     writeln('Enter a capital letter');
     readln(letter1);
     writeln('Enter another capital letter');
     readln(letter2);
     if letter1 < letter2 then
          writeln('The order is ',letter1,' ',letter2)
     else
          writeln('The order is ',letter2,' ',letter1);
end.
```

The condition *letter1* < *letter2* is used to establish whether or not the two characters are in the correct order; remember that the computer will use the characters' ASCII codes in order to do the checking.

Boolean Variables

Boolean *operators* were discussed earlier (in the section on *If..then..else*) and it is now time to look at a new type of variable, the *boolean variable*. A boolean variable can contain only one of two values and these must be the values *true* or *false*. Boolean variables can have values assigned to them just like any other kind of variable but we can only assign the values *true* and *false*. Some typical assignment statements for boolean variables are as follows: (where *NoSwaps* and *EndOfFile* have been previously declared as boolean variables.)

        NoSwaps : = false;   EndOfFile : = true;.

A boolean variable will normally have its value set by a condition in a program; if the condition evaluates to *true* then the variable will be set to the value *true*, otherwise it will be set to *false*.

For example, suppose that we want to write a program which will tell us whether or not a triangle contains a right-angle given the lengths of its three sides; we know from Pythagoras that in a right-angled triangle the square of the length of the longest side (the hypotenuse) is equal to the sum of the squares of the lengths of the other two sides. The classic right-angled triangle is the 3, 4, 5 triangle; using Pythagoras theorem this gives (3 * 3) + (4 * 4) = (5 * 5), that is,
 + 16 = 25, which is correct.

A program to do this, called Pythagoras, is shown on the next page and it uses the boolean variable *RightAngled*. *RightAngled* has its value set to *true* or *false* depending upon the *truth value* of the condition

        Hypotenuse * Hypotenuse = Side2 * Side2 + Side3 * Side3.

Note how *RightAngled* is used in the *if..then..else* statement which makes the decision. We write

        if RightAngled then etc.

rather than incorrectly as

        if RightAngled = true then etc.

If we wanted merely to check if the triangle was not right-angled we would write

        if not RightAngled then etc.

We would not write

        if RightAngled = false then etc.

In any event, writing it in the correct manner makes the program read much better and look more logical, thus making it easier to understand.

The word *not* is used to reverse the logic of the statement; in other words it makes the opposite true. Therefore, writing a statement such as

        if not not RightAngled

is the same as writing the statement

        if RightAngled

because the two *nots* cancel each other out.

```
program Pythagoras (input, output);
var
     Hypotenuse : integer;
     Side2 : integer;
     Side3 : integer;
     RightAngled : boolean;
begin
     write('Please give me the longest side ');
     readln(Hypotenuse);
     write('Please give me the other two sides ');
     readln(Side2, Side3);
     RightAngled := Hypotenuse * Hypotenuse = Side2 * Side2 + Side3 * Side3;
     if RightAngled then
          writeln('This triangle is a right-angled triangle')
     else
          writeln('This triangle is not a right-angled triangle');
end.
```

Simple Procedures

When writing a program it is often found that some piece of the program is used over and over again in different places in that program. Having to write out this piece of program many times is obviously time-consuming and space-wasting. What is called for is a mechanism whereby a piece of program - or *subprogram* - can be written out once and then called (or executed) by the main program whenever it is needed. This is exactly how procedures operate in Pascal.

Procedures are also useful when writing larger programs. They enable a program to be 'broken down' into smaller parts, each part (or procedure) being some identifiable task that the program has to carry out. The programmer can then concentrate solely on each of the procedures in turn, perhaps leaving the difficult or problematic ones until last - inspiration may come later! This approach to programming is a form of the so-called *divide and conquer* technique.

Any program written as a set of procedures will be inherently easier to read and understand than a monolithic program, that is, one written as a long set of instructions, as long as the procedures are given meaningful names.

The program below, called rocket1, draws a crude rocket shape using simple ASCII characters and then simulates the 'rocket' taking off. It uses three procedures called *DrawTop*, which is called only once, *DrawBox*, which is called three times, and *Exhaust*, which is called two hundred times! The rocket appears to take off because the *writeln* statements force the screen to scroll upwards.

```
program rocket1 (input, output);
var x : integer;
procedure DrawTop; {Declare procedure DrawTop}
    begin
        writeln('    /\  ');
        writeln('   /  \ ');
        writeln('  /    \');
        writeln('- - - - -');
    end;
procedure DrawBox; {Declare procedure DrawBox}
    begin
        writeln('- - - - - ');
        writeln('|        |');
        writeln('|        |');
        writeln('- - - - - ');
    end;
procedure Exhaust; {Declare procedure Exhaust}
    begin
        writeln(' |      | ');
        writeln;
    end;
begin{Main body of program}
    DrawTop;        {Call up procedure DrawTop}
    DrawBox;        {Call up procedure DrawBox}
    DrawBox;        {and again}
    DrawBox;        {and again}
    for x := 1 to 200 do {Call up procedure Exhaust 200 times}
        Exhaust;
end.
```

Notice that the procedures are declared after the variables and before the main body of the program and note that the structure of each procedure is exactly like the structure of a program, except that instead of using the word 'program', the word 'procedure' is used. The rules for procedure names are exactly the same as those for program names. (See chapter1).

The basic format of a *procedure* is thus

```
procedure name;
    begin
        statements
    end
```

One important result of using procedures is that the main body of the program is now extremely readable; the procedures are simply 'called-up' when they are needed and their internal 'workings' do not appear in the main body, thus simplifying it considerably.

In the main body of the program the procedures are 'called up' as and when required by simply giving their names. For example, the procedure *Drawbox* can be executed at any point in the program by inserting the word *Drawbox* at that point.

The program below, called SumUp, provides another example of the use of procedures. A procedure called *drawaline* (which draws a line!) is declared and is then called up at the various points in the program where a line has to be drawn.

```
program SumUp(input, output);      {User enters two numbers; the result is}
                                   {calculated and displayed in traditional fashion.}

var
      number1, number2 : real;
Procedure drawaline;               {Draws a line of 10 dashes.}
var i : integer;                   {The variable i is 'local' to the drawaline procedure.}
                                   {Details concerning local variables will be given later.}
begin
      for i : = 1 to 10 do         {Write 10 dashes then start new line.}
            write('-');
      writeln;
end;
begin
      writeln('Please enter the first number';
      readln(number1);
      writeln('Please enter the second number');
      readln(number2);
      writeln;
      writeln(number1:10:3);       {Write numbers in a field of 10 chars, to 3 d.p.}
      writeln(number2:10:3);
      drawaline;                   {Call procedure to draw 10 dashes.}
      writeln(number1 + number2:10:3);
      drawaline;                   {call procedure to draw 10 dashes.}
end.
```

If the numbers 123.7 and 300.67 were entered, the result would be as follows:

```
      1 2 3 . 7 0 0
_ _ _ 3 0 0 . 6 7 0
_ _ _ 4 2 4 . 3 7 0
```

Menu-Driven Programs

Many programs are classified as being *menu-driven*; this means that a choice of options is presented to the user, who then chooses an option by entering a specific character or number, as indicated by the menu. Normally, after the current option has been completed, control returns to the menu, which is once again displayed.

Menu-driven programs are easy to organize using procedures. The menu display can be written as a procedure and likewise each of the options can be written as procedures, or sets of procedures, if necessary. Choosing an option then becomes a simple matter of calling up the requisite procedure or procedures that make up that option.

To demonstrate this, the program MenuDemo, is shown below. This program uses two of the procedures, renamed *Triangle* and *Box*, from the earlier rocket program, along with three new procedures to display the menu, find out the user's choice and display a farewell message. These new procedures are called, respectively, *ShowMenu, UserChoice* and *Quit*.

```
program MenuDemo (input, output);
var
      Choice : integer;
procedure Triangle;
begin
      writeln('    /\    ');
      writeln('   /  \   ');
      writeln('  /      \');
      writeln('- - - - - -');
end;
procedure Box;
begin
      writeln('- - - - - - ');
      writeln('|          |');
      writeln('|          |');
      writeln('- - - - - - ');
end;
procedure Quit;
begin
      writeln('Goodbye. I hope you enjoyed this program.');
      writeln;
end;
procedure ShowMenu;
begin
      writeln('Do you wish to :-');
      writeln;
      writeln('(1) Draw a triangle?');
      writeln('(2) Draw a box?');
      writeln('(3) Draw a simple house?');
      writeln('(4) Quit the program?');
      writeln;
      write('Please choose - type 1, 2 ,3 or 4 and then press ENTER ');
end;
```

```
procedure UserChoice;
begin
      readln(Choice);
      if Choice = 1 then{Call up the Triangle procedure.}
            Triangle;
      if Choice = 2 then{Call up the Box procedure.}
            Box;
      if Choice = 3 then{Call up Triangle and then Box to draw a house.}
            begin
                  Triangle;
                  Box;
            end;
end;
begin {Main body of program.}
      repeat
            ShowMenu;
            UserChoice;
      until Choice = 4;
      Quit;
end.
```

Practice Programs

These programs should be keyed in and run to give more practice with the Pascal language. They should be studied until their operation is understood.

Program (a), which writes out a multiplication table, emphasizes the fact that a *writeln* statement can be used to perform arithmetic operations. When the expression $X * Table$ is encountered in the *writeln* statement, the values of X and *Table* will be looked up, multiplied together and then written out. This method can be used, where appropriate, to avoid writing assignment statements such as $Result := X * Table$, and then using the variable *Result* in the *writeln* statement. This is useful for writing out the values of results which do not need to be stored (in variables) in the computer when the program is running.

(a)

```
program TimesTable1 (input, output);
var
      X : integer;
      Table : integer;
begin
      write('Which table do you require? ');
      readln(Table);
      for X := 1 to 12 do
            writeln(X,' multiplied by ', Table,' = ',X * Table);
end.
```

Program (b) demonstrates the use of nested *for..to..do* loops for writing out a multiplication table in column form. The outer loop is traversed as many times as the number or rows required, and the inner loop is traversed as many times as the number of columns required. The value of X is calculated using the values of *Row* and *Column* in the assignment statement

$X := (Row - 1) * 4 + Column$. For example, if $Row = 1$ and $Column = 1$ then $X = 1$, that is, the value 1 is the correct value for X to have in the first column of the first row.

Tinker with this program by altering the limits of *Row* and *Column* in the two *for..to..do* statements. For example, try

        for Row : = 1 to 5

and

        for Column : = 1 to 3

to see what happens when you run the program.

(b)

```
program TimesTable2 (input, output);
var
    X : integer;
    Table : integer;
    Row : integer;
    Column : integer;
begin
    writeln('Which table do you require? ');
    readln(Table);
    for Row : = 1 to 3 do         {Specifies the number of rows - }
                                  {in this case, 3.}

    begin
        for Column : = 1 to 4 do      {Specifies the number of columns}
                                      {in each row - in this case, 4.}

        begin
            X : = (Row - 1) * 4 + Column;
            write(X:5,' x',Table:3,' =',X * Table:3);
        end;
        writeln;
    end;
end.
```

Program (c) extends the *case* statement example given in this chapter. The program is designed to calculate the number of days (result is stored in *DayNumber*) that have elapsed since the beginning of a year up to a given date in that year. The date is entered by the user. The program is quite straightforward but you should be aware of how leap years are calculated; a year is a leap year if it can be divided exactly by 4 but cannot be divided exactly by 100. The operator *mod* is used for this purpose. If the result of a *mod* operation is 0 then there must have been no remainder after the division was carried out; that is, the division must have been exact.

Note that a *validation check* is carried out on the value entered for *Month*. If this wasn't done then there could be values entered (such as 13) that would not be processed by the *case* statement and which would result in incorrect program operation. The validation check is carried out in the body of a *repeat..until* loop and this loop cannot be exited until a valid date is entered. Note how the validity of a month is checked. The boolean variable *ValidMonth* is set to the truth value of the compound condition

(Month > 0) and (Month < 13)

which is only true if a month is greater than 0 *and* is also less than 13. If either of these separate conditions is false then the whole condition will be false resulting in *ValidMonth* being given the value *false*.

As an exercise, write similar validation checks for the variable *Day*. This may be quite tricky; remember that not all months contain the same number of days and that February has 29 days if the year is a leap year.

(c)

```
program DayOfYear (input, output);
var
      Day : integer;
      Month : integer;
      Year : integer;
      DayNumber : integer;
      ValidMonth : boolean;
begin
      writeln('Please enter the day, month and year');
      writeln('For example, to enter 23rd of July, 1993');
      writeln('You would type in 23 7 1993 and then press ENTER');
      readln(Day, Month, Year);
      repeat                          {Validation check.}
          ValidMonth : = (Month > 0) and (Month < 13);
          if not ValidMonth then
              begin
                  writeln('Please re-enter date in correct format!');
                  readln(Day, Month, Year);
              end;
      until ValidMonth;               {End of validation check.}
      case Month of
          1 : DayNumber : = Day;
          2 : DayNumber : = Day + 31;
          3 : DayNumber : = Day + 59;
          4 : DayNumber : = Day + 90;
          5 : DayNumber : = Day + 121;
          6 : DayNumber : = Day + 151;
          7 : DayNumber : = Day + 182;
```

```
        8 : DayNumber : = Day + 212;
        9 : DayNumber : = Day + 242;
        10: DayNumber : = Day + 273;
        11: DayNumber : = Day + 303;
        12: DayNumber : = Day + 334;
    end;
    {Check - is it a leap year?}
    if Year mod 4 = 0 then
        if Year mod 100 < > 0 then
            if Month > 2 then
                DayNumber : = DayNumber + 1; {Add an extra day.}
    writeln('The date ',Day,' ',Month,' ',Year);
    writeln('is day number ',DayNumber,' of ',Year);
end.
```

Exercises

1 Rewrite program decision2 using only *if..then* statements in place of the *if..then..else* statements. Which program looks better?

2 Write a program using a *repeat..until* loop to read in 10 student marks from the keyboard. As each mark is input it must be checked to see whether it is a *PASS, FAIL* or *MERIT*.

Each mark is out of a possible 100 and is graded as follows:

0 – 39   FAIL

40 – 59   PASS

60 – 100 MERIT

Typical output for each mark:

Student Mark is 75, Grade is MERIT

3 Add extra checks to your program for question 2 so that impossible marks like
–3 and 123 are rejected by the program along with the message:

INVALID MARK - PLEASE RE-INPUT.

Note that the program should continue until 10 valid marks have been input and graded. Test your program thoroughly so that it works under all conditions.

4 Re-write your program for question 3 using a *while..do* loop in place of the *repeat..until* loop.

5 The following program, called SymbolCheck, is designed to establish whether a symbol being input is either a digit, a vowel or a consonant; if it is none of these then an error message is produced. The program contains nested *if..then..else* statements which, on a first reading, would appear to be

correct. The program, however, contains a bug (or error); if a digit is entered the output produced is of the form:

A digit was entered

Erroneous input!

The error message should not be printed in this case. Modify the program so that it operates correctly. Note that only uppercase letters will be considered by the program; lower case letters will be treated as erroneous input.

```
program SymbolCheck (input, output);
var
     symbol : char;
begin
     write('Please enter any symbol (i.e. any character) ');
     readln(symbol);
     if (symbol > = '0') and (symbol < = '9') then
          writeln('A digit was entered');
     if (symbol > = 'A') and (symbol < = 'Z') then
          if (symbol = 'A') or (symbol = 'E') or (symbol = 'I')
               or (symbol = 'O') or (symbol = 'U')
               then writeln('A vowel was entered')
          else
               writeln('A consonant was entered')
     else
          writeln('Erroneous Input!')
end.
```

6 Determine which of the boolean expressions below evaluate to *true* and which evaluate to *false*, given that $X = 1$, $Y = 2$ and $Z = 3$; *eof* and *eoln* are booleans and have the following values: eof = *true* and eoln = *false*.

(a) $(Y = Z)$ or $(Z > Y)$

(b) $(X + Y) > = Z$

(c) $(Y - X) < > (Z - Y)$

(d) $(X = 1)$ and $(Y = 2)$ and $(Z > 2)$

(e)   not $(X > 0)$

(f) $(X < > Y)$ or not $(Z > 0)$

(g)   not eoln and eof

(h)   not (not (eoln or eof))

(i) $(X < Y)$ and not eoln

(j)   not eof or eoln or $(X + Y + Z = 6)$

Assignment

Write a Pascal program to comply with the following:

When the program is run a menu is presented to the user; the menu should be of the form:

> Main Menu
> (1) Story
> (2) Test
> (3) Score
> (4) Quit
>
> Please choose (1,2,3 or 4)

It is intended that the user should choose options 1 to 4 in numerical order.

When the user chooses option (1) Story, an interesting short story (of say 20 lines at most) will appear on the monitor. The story should remain on-screen until the user presses the ENTER key.

Option (2) Test, will determine the user's understanding of the story presented in option 1 by asking questions about the story. The questions should be kept short and easy - multiple choice answers should be used. No more than 5 questions should be asked.

Option (3) Score, will inform the user of his/her test score.

Option (4) Quit, will halt the program after presenting a suitable 'goodbye' message to the user.

Notes:

(1)   Apart from option (4), after each option has been carried out the main menu should re-appear on-screen, that is, the program should be menu-driven. (Details are given in the section on procedures.)

(2)   Procedures are to be used effectively. Each option and the main menu should consist of one or more procedures.

(3)   Investigate the built-in functions and procedures of the version of Pascal that you are using in order to improve the 'look' of your program as it executes. For instance, there will probably be procedures to clear the screen and to place text at any position on the screen. In Turbo Pascal there is *clrscr* (clear screen) and *gotoxy* (place the cursor at the given screen co-ordinates). Other procedures may be available so that different combinations of colours can be used for text and text background. Your Pascal manual should provide the necessary details.

Chapter 3

Arrays

Simple Arrays

The kinds of variables we have met so far have been capable of holding one value only. These types of variables are referred to as as *simple data types*. Often we would like to have many values held in the computer's memory at the same time in order to process them in some way. For example, suppose that we wished to sort 200 numbers in memory. With the variable types we have met so far we would have to declare 200 variables to hold the 200 numbers. What if we wished to sort 10,000 numbers? 10,000 variables would be needed! In order to accomplish this we require *structured data types* which can store multiple values.

The simplest form of *data structure* is the array. An array variable is capable of holding as many values as we require; we can have arrays containing integers, arrays containing reals, arrays containing characters, etc. However, an array can only hold multiple values of the same type; hence it is impossible, for example, to have a single array containing both characters and reals.

The simplest form of array consists of only one dimension and so it resembles a list of values. To illustrate a *one-dimensional array*, consider the following array declaration:

NumberList : array[1..12] of integer;

This will declare the variable, *NumberList*, to be an array which can hold 12 integer values. Suppose some values are now allocated to the array, *NumberList*. *Numberlist* can be visualised as follows:

Array *NumberList*

Position	Value
[1]	35
[2]	123
[3]	7
[4]	3098
[5]	12
[6]	100
[7]	99
[8]	−123
[9]	1234
[10]	45
[11]	890
[12]	−9912

Each value in *NumberList* is referred to by using its positional value or *index*. For example, the value stored in position 7, that is, *the value referred to by the index 7*, is 99. The value stored in position 4 (that is, 3098) would be referred to as *NumberList[4]*. Suppose we wished to assign the value held in position 9 (that is, 1234) to an integer variable called *X*; we would use the statement:

```
X : = NumberList[9];
```

and if we wished to copy the contents of *Numberlist[11]* into *Numberlist[10]* we would write:

```
NumberList[10] : = NumberList[11];.
```

Similarly, the statement:

```
Numberlist[6] : = 25;
```

would ensure that *Numberlist[6]* contained the value 25.

If it is required to assign values to every element in an array then the best method to use is a loop. The *loop control variable* can be used as the *index* to each value. Program ArrayDemo1 demonstrates this technique.

```
program ArrayDemo1 (input, output);
var
      AccountNo : array[1..6] of integer;
      Balance : array[1..6] of real;
      Count : integer;  {Count is the loop control variable}
begin
      for Count : = 1 to 6 do    {Count is used as the index}
                                 {to each value in the array}
          begin
              writeln('Enter the Account Number');
              readln(AccountNo[Count]);
              writeln('Enter Balance');
              readln(Balance[Count]);
          end;
      writeln('Account No.        Balance');
      writeln;
      for Count : = 1 to 6 do
          writeln(AccountNo[Count]:11,Balance[Count]:15:2);
end.
```

AccountNo and *Balance* are both declared as arrays which can each hold 6 numbers. *AccountNo* is declared as an array of integers because account numbers consist of only whole numbers and *Balance* is declared as an array of reals because balances represent money which is normally written to 2 decimal places. Output from the program would be in the format shown on the next page:

Account No	Balance
12345	128.35
12355	1001.00
23456	9.99
90901	−12.50
32131	−11.65
77777	12345.67

Note that the output has been formatted to make it look neat. A simple extension to this program would be to incorporate a check to see which accounts were in the red (that is, below zero). See program ArrayDemo2 below.

```
program ArrayDemo2 (input, output);
var
      AccountNo : array[1..6] of integer;
      Balance : array[1..6] of real;
      Count : integer;
begin
      for Count : = 1 to 6 do
            begin
                  writeln('Enter the Account Number');
                  readln(AccountNo[Count]);
                  writeln('Enter Balance');
                  readln(Balance[Count]);
            end;
      writeln('Account No.      Balance');
      writeln;
      for Count : = 1 to 6 do
            writeln(AccountNo[Count]:11,Balance[Count]:15:2);
      writeln;{Leave 2 blank lines}
      writeln;
      for Count : = 1 to 6 do{List all accounts that are in the red}
            if Balance[Count] < 0 then
                  writeln(AccountNo[Count],' is in the red');
      end.
```

The next program, ArrayDemo3, shows one method of finding the largest number in an array (or list) of numbers.

```
program ArrayDemo3 (input, output);
var
    x, Largest : integer;
    NumberList : array[1..10] of integer;
begin
    for x : = 1 to 10 do        {Read in the numbers into the array}
        readln(NumberList[x]);
    Largest : = NumberList[1];
    for x : = 2 to 10 do        {Compare each number with the current Largest number}
            if NumberList[x] > Largest then
                Largest : = NumberList[x];
    writeln('The largest number is ',Largest);
end.
```

The program operates as follows:

The numbers are read into the array *NumberList* using a *for..to..do* loop. The variable *Largest* is then set to the value stored in *NumberList[1]*. At the start of this part of the program, *NumberList[1]* will contain the *current largest* value as the others have not yet been encountered. The rest of the numbers are now compared, one at a time, against the current largest value, which is held in the variable *Largest*, once again using a *for..to..do* loop. This comparison operation is carried out by the statement:

```
        if NumberList[x] > Largest then
            Largest : = NumberList[x];
```

which progressively compares *NumberList[2]* with *Largest*, *NumberList[3]* with *Largest* and so on until finally *NumberList[10]* is compared with *Largest*. The loop control variable, *x*, provides the index for each number in *NumberList* as *x* begins at 2 and ends at 10, going up in steps of 1. If any value in *NumberList* is found to be greater than the value held in *Largest* then *Largest* is set to that value in *NumberList*. When the loop has been executed 9 times, the variable *Largest* contains the largest value in the list.

Introduction to Sorting - The BubbleSort

There are many occasions when it is necessary to sort data into some kind of order. For example, the assignment at the end of this chapter requires the median of a set of numbers to be determined. To find the median value requires sorting the numbers into ascending order of size (that is, smallest first) and then locating the middle number. In more complex situations, such as file handling in data processing applications, sorting is a necessity. Many file handling techniques employed are dependent upon having files that have previously been sorted into order.

In addition to sorting into ascending order, data can be sorted into descending order of size, that is, with largest number first. If the list of values 21, 3, 56, 2, –9, 5, 3 was sorted into ascending order then the result would be:

$$-9, \qquad 2, \qquad 3, \qquad 3, \quad 5, \qquad\qquad 21, \qquad 56$$

and if they were sorted into descending order the result would be:

$$56, \qquad 21, \qquad 5, \qquad 3, \quad 3, \qquad\qquad 2, \qquad -9.$$

Many techniques are available for sorting data and one of the simplest methods is known as the *BubbleSort*. The idea behind the BubbleSort is a simple one. The numbers to be sorted are stored in an array, and then, starting at the beginning of the array, each pair of consecutive numbers is examined. If they are in correct order they are left alone but if they are in incorrect order they are swapped around; that is, the two numbers change positions in the array. To illustrate this method, consider the set of numbers given previously:

21	First, 21 and 3 are examined and found to be in the wrong order
3	so they swap positions giving the next list:
56	
2	
–9	
5	
3	

3	
21	21 and 56 are compared; they don't need to be swapped around.
56	56 and 2 are now examined; they must be swapped around
2	giving the next list:
–9	
5	
3	

3	
21	
2	
56	56 and –9 are examined; they must be swapped around giving
–9	the next list:
5	
3	

3	
21	
2	
–9	
56	56 and 5 are examined and swapped around giving the next list:
5	
3	

3
21
2
–9
5
56   56 and 3 are examined and swapped around giving the next
3   list:

3
21
2
–9
5
3
56

The entire list of numbers has now been examined but the numbers are still not in order. The above process must be repeated again and again until the numbers are in order. Each traversal of the list is called a *pass*. Try the method yourself on paper to determine how many more passes will be required to sort the list completely. The process seems slow and long-winded but, fortunately, a computer can carry out the task much faster.

The problem of how to program the computer to decide whether or not another pass is required, or to state it more simply, to decide whether or not the numbers are now completely sorted, is easily solved; we will use a *boolean* variable called *NoSwaps*. At the commencement of each pass we will set the variable *NoSwaps* to be *true;* if at any time during the pass two values have to be swapped around, because they are in the wrong order, *NoSwaps* will be set to *false*. A further pass will be commenced only if *NoSwaps* is *false*. If, at the end of a pass, *NoSwaps* is found to be *true*, then, during that pass, the numbers must have all been in the correct order and hence fully sorted.

Only one detail remains and that is how to swap two values around. As usual we will use the loop control variable (in this case the variable *x*) to keep track of where we are in the array (which we will call *list*). So, the current value in the array will be identified as *list[x]* and the next value in the array following *list[x]* must be *list[x+1]*. For example, when we first start examining values in the list and *x* is equal to 1 then *list[x]* and *list[x+1]* actually refer to *list[1]* and *list[2]*; when *x* is equal to 2 then *list[x]* and *list[x+1]* refer to *list[2]* and *list[3]* and so on. To swap two values around now amounts to making sure that *list[x]* contains the value that was in *list[x+1]* and that *list[x+1]* contains the value that was in *list[x]*.

At first sight, the following statements seem to be sufficient to carry out the swapping operation:

```
list[x] : = list[x + 1];
list[x + 1] : = list[x];
```

but careful consideration reveals that after these instructions have been carried out, both *list[x]* and *list[x+1]* contain whatever value was originally in *list[x+1]*! Whatever was in *list[x]* is lost because the first statement,

list[x] := *list[x+1]*, copies whatever was in *list[x+1]* into *list[x]*. Therefore, the contents of *list[x]* must be stored temporarily in another variable, prior to being set to the value in *list[x+1]*. We will call this extra variable, *temp*.

The statements required to carry out a swap are thus:

```
temp : = list[x];          {make a copy of list[x] in temp}
list[x] : = list[x + 1];   {copy list[x + 1] into list[x]}
list[x + 1] : = temp;      {copy the original contents of list[x]}
                           {(which are now in temp) into list[x + 1]}
```

The complete sorting program, called BubbleSort, is now given.

```
program BubbleSort (input, output);
var
      list : array[1..10] of real;
      x : integer;
      temp : real;
      NoSwaps : boolean;
begin
      for x: = 1 to 10 do        {Enter the data.}
            begin
                  writeln('enter number ',x);
                  readln(list[x]);
            end;
      repeat                     {Sort the data.}
            NoSwaps : = true;
            for x : = 1 to 9 do    {Only 9 comparisons are required for 10 numbers}
                  begin
                        if list[x] > list[x + 1] then
                              begin    {Do a swap.}
                                    temp : = list[x];
                                    list[x] : = list[x + 1];
                                    list[x + 1] : = temp;
                                    NoSwaps: = false;    {Indicate that a swap has been made.}
                              end;
                  end;
      until NoSwaps;{If NoSwaps is false go back and do another pass.}
      writeln;
      writeln('Here is your sorted data');
      writeln;
      for x : = 1 to 10 do
            writeln(list[x]:10:2);
end.
```

Note the condition *until NoSwaps* (meaning 'until NoSwaps is true') in the *repeat..until* loop. It is in effect saying, 'repeat the loop until a pass has been made during which there were *no swaps*'.

In its present form the BubbleSort above is not very fast. One way of making the BubbleSort faster is to note that, after the first pass, the largest number is in its correct position at the bottom of the list. After the second pass, the second largest number is in its correct position (one place off bottom of the list), and so on. This means that it is not necessary to examine every pair of data items in the list during every pass; only the first pass requires that 9 pairs of numbers are examined. (Remember that the sort given above will sort 10 numbers, thus requiring 9 pairs of numbers to be compared.) During the second pass only 8 pairs of numbers need be examined, during the third pass only 7 pairs of numbers need be examined, etc.

The next program, BubbleSort2, includes this enhancement. It uses a constant called *Size* and a new variable called *p*. This variable, *p*, is decremented (reduced by 1) after each pass. Initially, *p* is set to the value of the constant, *Size*, which specifies how many numbers are to be sorted (10 in the current program). You can sort as many numbers as you wish by altering the value of *Size* in the program; try putting *Size* = *20* , for example; and note how *Size* is used in the loop control statements of the program. The first pass compares *p* – *1* (that is, 9) pairs of numbers and on each subsequent pass *p* is reduced by *1* using the statement

```
p := p - 1;
```

in the *repeat..until* loop. This effectively shortens the list by 1 after each pass.

```
program BubbleSort2 (input, output);
                        {Speeds up BubbleSort by reducing the length of}
                        {the unsorted list by 1 after each pass.}
    const
        Size = 10;        {Specify the size of the array.}
    var
        list : array[1..Size] of real;
        x, p : integer;
        temp : real;
        NoSwaps : boolean;
    begin
        for x := 1 to Size do
            begin
                write('enter number ',x,' ');
                readln(list[x]);
            end;
        writeln;
        for x := 1 to Size do
                writeln('no. ',x,' is ',list[x]);
        writeln;
        writeln('Press the ENTER key to see your numbers in correct order');
        readln;
        p := Size;
```

```
        repeat
            NoSwaps : = true;
            for x : = 1 to p − 1 do
                begin
                    if list[x] > list[x + 1] then
                        begin
                            temp : = list[x];
                            list[x] : = list[x + 1];
                            list[x + 1] : = temp;
                            NoSwaps : = false;
                        end;
                end;
            p : = p − 1   {Reduce list length by 1.}
        until NoSwaps;
        writeln;
        for x : = 1 to Size do
            writeln(list[x]:10:2);
    end.
```

It should be noted that sorting is not restricted to numerical data; characters, character strings, files of records etc. can all be sorted. A program to demonstrate how character strings can be sorted is given later in this chapter.

The Read Procedure

So far, whenever data has been entered from the keyboard, it has been done using the *readln* procedure. The *read* procedure is an alternative to the *readln* procedure and should be avoided, if possible, because of its ability to cause 'peculiar program action' when used by inexperienced programmers. There are, however, occasions when *read* should be used, for example in file processing (to be discussed at length, later), for which it was designed, and for situations where *readln* is unsuitable. A typical application for the *read* procedure is character processing. Before illustrating such an application, it will be worth comparing the ways that *read* and *readln* operate.

The *read* and *readln* procedures both perform the same operation of reading data into some variable or variables; the statements

    read(ch)   and   readln(ch)

each cause a character to be read into the variable *ch* (declared as a *char* variable). The difference between them is that after *readln(ch)* has been carried out (by pressing the *ENTER* key) it will ignore any extra characters that have been typed in. If the characters 'ab' are typed in then the character 'a' would be stored in the variable *ch* and the character 'b' would be ignored and lost forever. In other words, after reading in the amount of data intended, in this case one character, *readln* will jump to the end of the current data line. Any future data to be read in must be entered on a new data line.

Read, on the other hand, will not jump to the end of the data line after reading in a character; in the above situation, the character 'a' would be read into *ch* and the character 'b' would remain in the current data line waiting to be read by the next *read* or *readln* statement encountered in the program. This presents problems for the unwary; extra characters typed in by mistake at one point in a program may be read in by another statement later in the program. Unexpected program action may result.

It should now be clear that if we wish to process strings of characters typed in on the same line, the *readln* procedure will not do because we would have to press *ENTER* after every character; thus, each character would have to be entered on a separate line. The *eoln* identifier is also necessary for most character processing situations because it is used to detect when the end of a line of text has been reached. (See next section.)

Eof and Eoln

There are times when it is necessary to detect the end of a file; the mechanism for doing this is to have the end of a file specially marked with a so-called *end-of-file marker*. In computers using the DOS operating system, the end-of-file marker is the *control-z* (or *ctrl-z*) character. This character can be generated from the keyboard by holding down the *control* (*ctrl*) key and then pressing the *z* key once; the *ctrl* key can then be released. Computers using operating systems other than DOS may employ different end-of-file markers.

In Pascal programs, the identifier *eof* is used when we wish to detect the end of a file. The Pascal identifier *eof* is of type boolean and so it can contain one of the values *true* or *false*. If the end of a file is detected then *eof* is set to the value *true*; if the end of a file has not been detected then *eof* will be set to *false*.

At this point you may be wondering why files are being included in this discussion. The reason is as follows. If we wish to process data, character by character, then we must enter it from the keyboard. The computer's operating system views the keyboard as a special type of file. We could keep on entering data from this keyboard file forever, but there will obviously come a time when we will wish to stop. This is achieved by entering *ctrl-z*. Pascal will recognise this special character as the end-of-file marker and will consider that we have finished our data entry.

Eoln is also a boolean identifier and so it operates in a similar manner to *eof*. The identifier *eoln* is used in Pascal programs when we wish to detect the *end of a line;* that is, *eoln* will have the value *true* when the end of a line of text is reached, otherwise it will have the value *false*. In a keyboard file, the end-of-a-line marker can be inserted using the *ENTER* or *RETURN* key. Note that *eoln* can only be used with *text* files.

The following program illustrates a character processing task; a piece of text is to be read into the computer via the keyboard, one character at a time. The program has to count the number of words, the number of spaces between the words and the number of lines of text that have been input. The program is designed to show how *read*, *eof* and *eoln* can be used.

```
program CharCount (input, output);
var
      ThisChar, LastChar : char;
      words, spaces, lines : integer;
begin
                           {Initialize variables.}
      words : = 0;
      spaces : = 0;
```

```
            lines : = 0;
            LastChar : = ' ';                 {LastChar is set to a space.}
                                                     {Begin processing characters.}
            read(ThisChar);
            while not eof do {End of file (eof) is indicated by entering ctrl-z.}
                  begin
                        if ThisChar = ' ' then
                              if LastChar < > ' ' then    {If last character was a space}
                                                                {don't add 1 to the word count.}
                                    begin
                                          spaces : = spaces + 1;
                                          words : = words + 1;
                                    end
                              else
                                    spaces : = spaces + 1;
                        if eoln then
                              begin
                                    lines : = lines + 1;
                                    words : = words + 1;
                              end;
                        LastChar : = ThisChar;                   {Save last character for}
                                                                 {'space' check.}
                        read(ThisChar);                          {Get next character.}
                  end;
            writeln('Number of words = ',words,' Number of spaces = ',spaces);
            writeln('Number of lines = ',lines);
      end.
```

The idea behind the program is as follows. Characters are read into the computer one at a time and stored in the variable *ThisChar;* if a character is a 'space' then 1 is added to the space count (using the variable *spaces*). Words are counted by recognising that the end of each word will be followed by a space or an end-of-line marker. To overcome the possibility of a word being followed by two or more spaces, the program only adds 1 to the word count if the previous character was not a space. The previous character input is stored in the variable *LastChar*. The word count is stored in the variable *words*. The variable *lines* stores the line count and this is increased by 1 (that is, incremented) every time the end-of-line character is encountered in the file. The end of the file is reached when *ctrl-z* is entered.

The results of entering the following piece of text:

> *The quick brown fox*
> *jumped over the moon*
> *all on a summer's day.*
> *ctrl-z*

would be:

    Number of words = 13 Number of spaces = 10
    Number of lines = 3.

Note that the program will operate incorrectly if leading spaces or trailing spaces are placed on any of the lines of text. As many spaces as you want can be entered between the words on each line. For example, *The   quick brown   fox* is a valid line of text. *Ctrl-z* must be entered on the line following the last line of text.

Character Arrays

So far we have dealt with arrays consisting of numbers (integers and reals), but it is common to have to write programs which manipulate arrays containing data of other types. An array of characters, often referred to as a *character string*, can be declared in the usual way, but, depending upon the version of Pascal you are using, you may have to include the word *packed* in the array declaration. Turbo Pascal does not require the word *packed* but will accept it if it is included.

The program below, called CharArray, demonstrates how to declare a *packed array* of four characters. Characters are read into the array and are then written out in different ways; initially, each character is written out on a separate line, and secondly, the characters are written out in the reverse order of being read in. So, if the characters 'abcd' were read in, the output would be:

    a
    b
    c
    d

followed by

    dcba

Note the use of a *readln* to remove any extra characters that may have been typed in. This is not really necessary in this program but in a program which had another *read* statement to follow, it would ensure that no unwanted characters could be read by mistake.

```
program CharArray (input, output);
var
     CharString : packed array[1..4] of char;
     x : integer;
begin
     for x := 1 to 4 do        {Read in each character.}
         read(CharString[x]);
     readln;{Flush the input buffer to remove extra characters that may have been entered.}
     for x := 1 to 4 do        {Write each character on a new line.}
         writeln(CharString[x]);
     for x := 4 downto 1 do {Write characters in reverse order on same line.}
         write(CharString[x]);
     writeln;
end.
```

Character Strings

This section discusses an extension to Standard Pascal which is becoming commonplace. If, however, the version of Pascal you are using does not support the type *string* then please either skip this topic altogether or consult your Pascal manual to see which facilities are available to you for manipulating character strings.

A *string* (short for character string) is simply a collection or *array* of characters. String variables are needed to hold non-numerical data such as names and addresses. The programmer can, as explained in the previous section, declare variables which are arrays of characters. One such variable declaration is as follows:

```
var
    name : packed array[1..15] of char;
```

which will allow a name of up to 15 characters to be stored in memory. The problem with this approach (which may be the only approach in some versions of Pascal) is that in order to manipulate data in this form it is necessary to deal with it on a *character by character* basis. Really, what we would like to do is deal with the data on a *word by word* basis, which is a much more natural way for us.

Using the variable type *string,* the above variable declaration can be rewritten as:

```
var
    name : string[15];
```

which will allow *name* to be treated as a single word containing 15 characters. Similarly, an array or list of 12 names could be declared as follows:

```
var
    namelist : array[1..12] of string[20];.
```

This will set aside enough memory to hold an array which can store 12 names, each of which can be up to 20 characters long. In practice, strings can normally be declared to hold up to 255 characters each.

The program below, StringDemo, sets up a number of product lines (only 5 in order to keep the program short) of the kind that would be encountered in a supermarket. Each product has a unique code by which it can be identified and also a description or name. Note that spaces are allowed in strings so that we can have product names such as 'washing powder'. Obviously, in the case of a real supermarket, each product line would need to contain much more data, such as that relating to cost, size, colour (if necessary) and so on.

The program acts like a look-up facility; the user types in a product code, the codes are then searched through using a loop and if the product code is found then the associated product name is displayed. If the input code does not exist in the product code array then nothing is displayed. The program repeats until the user decides that no more codes are to be looked up.

```
program StringDemo (input, output);
var
    InputCode, x : integer;
    ProductCode : array[1..5] of integer;
    ProductName : array[1..5] of string[15];
    reply : char;
```

```
begin
    {Set up the product lines.}
    ProductCode[1] := 1111; ProductName[1] := 'Washing Powder';
    ProductCode[2] := 2112; ProductName[2] := 'Baked Beans';
    ProductCode[3] := 3113; ProductName[3] := 'Tomato Soup';
    ProductCode[4] := 4114; ProductName[4] := 'Tea Bags';
    ProductCode[5] := 5115; ProductName[5] := 'Skimmed Milk';
    repeat
        writeln('Please enter the Product Code');
        readln(InputCode);
        for x := 1 to 5 do
            {Search the product codes looking for a match.}
            if InputCode = ProductCode[x] then
                writeln('Product name is ',ProductName[x]);
        writeln;
        writeln('Do you wish to enter another Product Code?');
        readln(reply);
    until (reply = 'N') or (reply = 'n');
end.
```

Note that the information relating to each product is set up using assignment statements. It would be tedious to type them all in at run time each time the program is executed! Note also that the product names must be enclosed in single quotes, just like single characters are in statements such as *until (reply = 'N') or (reply = 'n')*. In a real application, the data relating to the products would be held in files stored on disk and read into computer memory when required to be processed. (Files will be dealt with in a later chapter.)

Sorting Character Strings

As stated previously, character strings can be sorted in exactly the same way as numerical data. The earlier section on sorting demonstrated the BubbleSort method. The program below, called SortStrings, is based on the enhanced BubbleSort program, that is, *BubbleSort2*, from that earlier section, and sorts a set of names into ascending order.

The only changes required are those relating to the variables used for storing the character strings. Thus, an array of strings must be declared instead of an array of integers; the new declaration is

```
names : array[1..Size] of string[10];
```

where each string is declared to hold a maximum of 10 characters. Also, our temporary 'swap' variable, *temp*, must now be declared as being of type string[10]. Once again, the constant named *Size*, can be changed to the value of the number of strings that are to be sorted.

```
program SortStrings (input, output);
const
    Size = 10;        {Specify the size of the array.}
var
    names : array[1..Size] of string[10];
    x, p : integer;
    temp : string[10];        {Used when a swap is made.}
    NoSwaps : boolean;
begin
    for x := 1 to Size do      {Read in the names.}
        begin
            write('enter name - 10 characters maximum ',x,' ');
            readln(names[x]);
        end;
    writeln;
    write('Press enter to see your names sorted ');
    readln;
    writeln;
    p := Size;
    repeat
        NoSwaps := true;
        for x := 1 to p - 1 do
            begin
                if names[x] > names[x + 1] then
                    begin
                        temp := names[x];
                        names[x] := names[x + 1];
                        names[x + 1] := temp;
                        NoSwaps:= false;
                    end;
            end;
        p := p - 1; {Reduce list length by 1.}
    until NoSwaps;
    for x := 1 to Size do
        writeln(names[x]);
end.
```

Note that if you enter a name of more than 10 characters (either accidently or wilfully), the extra characters will be ignored. For example, typing in the name *Larry the Lamb* will produce the string *Larry The* . The *readln* procedure is more suitable than the *read* procedure in this application.

Exercises

1 Modify program ArrayDemo3 so that the smallest value in the array *Number-List* is found as well as the largest.

2 Write a program to find the average of a set of 15 numbers stored in an array of reals called *NumberSet*.

3 Write a program which reads 6 numbers into an array called *first* and then copies those numbers *in reverse order* into an array called *second*. Write out the contents of both arrays.

4 Modify the BubbleSort program so that 15 numbers can be sorted into descending order.

5 Write a program which declares two arrays: one to store 10 names (that is, an array of strings), the other to store 10 numbers (that is, an array of integers) representing the ages of the people named in the strings. For example, the data might look like this:

Position	Array Names	Array Ages
1	John	24
2	Angela	18
3	Daisy	19
4	Rachel	18
5	Michael	18
6	David	17
7	Maxine	23
8	Christopher	4
9	Jim	44
10	Joan	37

The program must sort the names into order and at the same time make sure that the ages are sorted accordingly so that the correct positions are maintained. So, for example, Rachel is currently in position 4 in the *names* array and her age is in position 4 in the *ages* array. After sorting, Rachel will be in position 10 in the *names* array and her age (18) will be in position 10 in the *ages* array.

6 Modify program StringDemo so that if the user types in a product code that does not exist in the array *ProductCode* a suitable message will be displayed. Hint: use a boolean variable called *ProductFound* to determine whether or not the product code exists.

7   Expand program StringDemo so that it contains at least 12 product lines and each product line also contains data relating to cost and size. Use procedures to make the program more readable. When a product is found all of the data relating to it should be displayed.

8   Write a program which stores telephone numbers and associated names and addresses. By typing in a name the user should be presented with that person's telephone number and address. A suitable message should be displayed if the name asked for does not exist. Note: telephone numbers are too large to be stored in normal integer variables. You may find that your version of Pascal supports *long integers* (*longint* in Turbo Pascal); check your manual to find out. If this fails then use reals formatted to display values to 0 decimal places.

9   Many names, although they sound the same, may be spelled in different ways; this can cause problems in information retrieval systems. For example, if trying to locate data relating to someone with the name 'Waites', typing in 'Waits' or 'Whaites' would be unlikely to locate the required record. One way to get around this problem is to convert each name to a *Soundex Code*. Details of this are given below:

(a)   the first letter of the name becomes the first letter of the code

(b)   all subsequent vowels, and the letters *H, W* and *Y* are ignored

(c)   double letters are replaced by a single instance of the letter

(d)   the remaining letters are replaced by values according to the table below:

Letter	Code
BFPV	1
CGJKQSXZ	2
DT	3
L	4
MN	5
R	6

(e)   the code is restricted to four characters in length

(f)   if the code contains less than four characters, it is padded with trailing zeros.

Write a program to read in a surname and write out the equivalent code. For example,

Morton	becomes	M635
Morten	becomes	M635
Norton	becomes	N635

Waites	becomes	W320
Whaites	becomes	W320
Waits	becomes	W320

10 The following table illustrates the *Morse Code:*

A	.-	N	-.
B	-...	O	- - -
C	-.-.	P	.- -.
D	-..	Q	- -.-
E	.	R	.-.
F	..-.	S	...
G	- -.	T	-
H	....	U	..-
I	..	V	...-
J	.- - -	W	.- -
K	-.-	X	-..-
L	.-..	Y	-.- - -
M	- -	Z	- - ..

Write a program to read in a word (or a sentence if you wish) and output it in Morse Code.

Assignment

Write a simple statistical package in Pascal.

Given a set of numbers stored in an array (the numbers to be read in at run time) the program has to compute the following statistics:

the number of values (a count of how many numbers were input)

the maximum (that is, largest) value

the minimum (that is, smallest) value

the mean (or average) value

the median (or middle) value.

The set of numbers, which must be reals, should be input by the user at run time. The user should be allowed to decide how many numbers are going to be input.

Notes:

The *mean* is calculated by adding together all of the numbers which were input (that is, the total) and then dividing the total by the count of how many numbers were input. For example, suppose the following 7 numbers were input:

> 2, 3, 5, 2, 3, 7, 6

then their total would be $2+3+5+2+3+7+6$ which equals 28 and their mean (or average) would be 28 divided by 7, which equals 4.

The *median* is determined by sorting the numbers into order and then choosing the middle value. If there is no middle value, as in the case of an even number of numbers being input, then the value next to the middle of the list can be used as the median. For example, given the following list of numbers:

> 1, 2, 3, 6, 7, 10, 11, 15, 16, 20

the middle of the list is in between the numbers 7 and 10 and so either the 7 or the 10 would do as the median. (The number 7 would probably be used.) If the list contained the following numbers:

> 1, 3, 5, 6, 9, 11, 12, 15, 24

the middle value, and hence the median, would have to be the number 9.

The position of the middle value in the sorted list can be calculated as follows: Add 1 to the count of how many numbers were input and then divide this figure by 2 (that is, *div* by 2).

Procedures must be used to make the program more readable and manageable; for instance the BubbleSort program could be rewritten as a procedure, as could the program statements required to find the median value. As a guide, the programmer will probably have to write the following procedures:

> procedure EnterData
> procedure SortData
> procedure FindMaxAndMinValues {Use the sorted data}
> procedure CalculateMean
> procedure CalculateMedian
> procedure DisplayStatistics.

Chapter 4

Functions and Procedures

Standard Functions

Invariably, a high level language comes complete with a library of functions (and also procedures); useful, pre-written routines that are available to the programmer and which can be used without any knowledge of the code that they contain. All the programmer needs to know is what type of *parameter* or *argument* the function needs and what kind of result the function *returns*.

A parameter is simply a value that is supplied to the function. In case this sounds daunting, a simple example should make things clear.

A common operation in mathematics is finding the square of a number (for example, the square of 7 is 7*7, which equals 49) and because this operation is so common there is a built-in Pascal function that can be used to carry it out. The function is called *sqr*, which of course is short for square, and it requires a parameter that is either a real or an integer; a character would be unacceptable as an argument because it would make no sense to try and find the square a character! The result returned by the function will be a value of the same type as the parameter it was called with. That is, if *sqr* is called with an integer parameter then the result will be an integer; if *sqr* is called with a real parameter then the result will be a real.

Having declared a variable called *result* (as either a real or integer) to find the result of squaring 7 we would write:

```
result : = sqr(7);
```

where the parameter is 7 and, as is the case with all functions, is enclosed in round brackets following the name of the function. The result of squaring 7, that is, 49, will be stored in *result*. It should be seen that using or calling a function is similar to calling a procedure. The difference is that a function *always* returns a value; a procedure may, or may not return a value, the choice is left up to the programmer.

Mathematical Functions

Standard Pascal contains many functions and most of them are mathematical. A list of Standard Pascal's mathematical functions is given on the next page, and shows the type of parameter required and the type of result returned by each one.

Function	Description	Parameter	Result
abs	Gives the absolute value of parameter	real/int	real/int
exp	Raises *e* to the power of the parameter	real/int	real
ln	Gives the natural log of the parameter	real/int	real
sqr	Squares the parameter	real/int	real/int
sqrt	Finds the square root of the parameter (which must be a positive value)	real/int	real
round	Rounds off parameter to nearest whole number	real	integer
trunc	Gives whole number part of parameter	real	integer
arctan	Gives arctan of the argument	real/int	real
cos	Gives the cosine of the parameter	real/int	real
sin	Gives the sine of the parameter	real/int	real
odd	Returns *true* if parameter is odd otherwise returns *false*.	integer	boolean

Note that *arctan*, *cos* and *sin* require the parameter to be a value given in radians and not degrees. There are (2 * Pi) radians to 360 degrees; thus, one radian is approximately 57 degrees.

To convert degrees into radians use the following formula (which is written in Pascal):

    R := (2 * Pi * N)/360   where   Pi = 3.1418...etc.

                                              N is the number of degrees

                                and   R is the number of radians

To convert from radians to degrees the formula is:

    N := (R * 360)/(2 * Pi).

Functions For Ordinal Data Types

Ordinal data types are so called because they consist of data items that can be placed in some unique order. For example, the letters of the alphabet form an ordinal set; the first letter is 'a', the second letter is 'b' and so on up to 'z' which is the 26th letter. With an ordinal type every value (except the last) has a unique successor and every value (except the first) has a unique predecessor. In the alphabet, the successor of 'b' is 'c' and the predecessor of 'b' is 'a'.

In Pascal, the ordinal types are integers, chars and booleans. The integers can be listed in order from –32786 through to 32767 (*maxint*). A subset of the set of integers is the set of positive integers, that is, the numbers 1, 2, 3, 4, 5 up to 32767. The order of the boolean values is *false* followed by *true*, and the order of the character (char) values follows their order in the ASCII code (or whichever code is used by the computer). The lower case letters (a, b, c ... z) and the upper case letters (A, B, C .. Z) form ordinal sets within the ASCII set thereby maintaining correct alphabetical ordering when using ordinal functions.

In the ASCII code 'a' has the value 97, 'b' has the value 98 and so on up to 'z' which has the value 122; the letter 'A' has the value 65, 'B' has the value 66 and so on up to 'Z' which has the value 90. There is a simple relationship between upper and lower case letters in the ASCII set. To convert a lower case letter to its upper case form, for example to convert 'a' to 'A', simply subtract 32 from its code, that is, $97 - 32 = 65$. To convert an upper case letter to its lower case form, e.g. to convert 'A' to 'a' simply add 32 to its code, that is, $65 + 32 = 97$.

Standard Pascal's ordinal functions are listed below:

Function	Description
pred	Returns the predecessor of the parameter, for example, given the parameter 12 the result will be 11
succ	Returns the successor of the parameter, for example, given the parameter 'f' the result will be 'g'
ord	Returns the ordinal value (or position) of the parameter, for example, given the parameter 'a' the result will be 97, which is the parameter's position in the ASCII set.
chr	This is the inverse of ord. It returns the character having the ordinal value given as the parameter, for example, given the parameter 97 the result will be 'a'.

Miscellaneous (Non Standard) Functions

Consultation of the manual for the version of Pascal you are using will probably reveal a wealth of non-standard functions that can be incorporated into your programs. One very useful, non-standard function is the *random* function which generates a random number from a range of numbers which the programmer specifies. For example, random(6) will generate one number from the set of numbers 0,1,2,3,4,5 and random(10) will generate one number from the set of numbers 0,1,2,3,4,5,6,7,8,9. Each number in the set is as equally likely to be generated as any other number in the set.

The generation of random numbers forms the basis of many statistical programs and games of chance; throwing a die or tossing a coin can be easily simulated. For example, to simulate the throwing of a die the following statement could be used:

```
DieThrow := random(6) + 1;
```

where random(6) will randomly produce a number between 0 and 5; adding 1 to the result will therefore produce a number between 1 and 6. The program below, RandDemo, simulates throwing a die 40 times. This program is written in Turbo Pascal and requires the random number generator to be initialized with a random value or *seed*; this is accomplished by calling up the built-in procedure *randomize* before any calls to the *random* function are made.

```
program RandDemo (output);
var
     x: integer;
const
     number = 6;
begin
     randomize;{Initialize random number generator.}
     writeln('Here are 40 throws of a die');
     writeln;
     for x := 1 to 40 do
          write(random(number) + 1,' ');
       writeln;
end.
```

The next program, called DiceGame, simulates a simple game of chance for one player and the computer. The rules are as follows:

two dice are thrown;

if the dice are the same or the total of the two dice equals 7 then the player wins, otherwise the computer wins.

```
program DiceGame (input, output);
var
     die1, die2, x : integer;
begin
     randomize;
     for x: = 1 to 5 do
          begin
               die1 := random(6) + 1;
               die2 := random(6) + 1;
               writeln('First throw is a ',die1,' Second throw is a ',die2);
               if ((die1 + die2) = 7) or (die1 = die2) then
                    writeln('Player wins')
               else
                    writeln('Computer wins');
          end;
end.
```

The game is played 5 times. The integer variables *die1* and *die2* are used to store the two randomly generated die scores and an *if..then..else* statement is used to determine the winner of the game. Note that there are two conditions in the *if..then..else* statement and that each one is placed in brackets. The two conditions are then *'or'ed* together to form a compound condition.

User-Created Functions

Often, a programmer needs a function that is not readily available and so has to write it from scratch. Once written, however, that function can be added to the existing library of functions and used in the same way as a standard function.

The program below, called MaxVal, contains a function called *max* that is called with two parameters or arguments and which determines the maximum or larger of the two; if it is called with the values 12 and 34, for instance, it will return the result 34.

```
program MaxVal (input, output);
var
     x, y : integer;
function max(a,b : integer) : integer; {Declare the max function}
begin
     if a > = b then
          max := a
     else
          max := b;
end;
begin    {Main body}
     readln(x,y);
     writeln('Maximum value is ',max(x,y));
end.
```

A function is declared by using the word *function* followed by the name of the function; in this case it is called *max*. Any parameters that are required are placed, along with their type, in brackets after the function name. This function needs two integer parameters *a* and *b*. The type of the result then follows; in this case the returned result will be of type *integer*.

As with procedures, the body of the function is placed between the words *begin* and *end*. The value to be returned must be assigned to the function name and so in the above function the maximum value is assigned to *max*, that is, *max* contains either *a* or *b*, whichever is the larger. If *a = b* then either value will do.

Note that, in the main body of the program, *max* is called with the variables *x* and *y* which have been entered by the user, yet in the function declaration, *max* uses the variables *a* and *b*. What happens is that the values in *x* and *y* are copied into *a* and *b* in order to be used by the function. This means that a function can be called up with *any* parameters as long as they are of the correct type. For example, to find the maximum of 3 and 7, *max* could be called with *max(3,7)* and 7 would be returned; the 3 would be copied into *a* and the 7 would be copied into *b* for processing by the function. Should it be required that the value returned from a function be stored in a variable then a statement such as

```
BiggerOne := max(FirstNumber, SecondNumber);
```

would be used. In this case, the variable *BiggerOne* would be declared as an integer, in order to match the type of the returned value. (Actually, a real variable would do just as well; see the section on assignment compatibility.)

The format of a *function* is

> function **name(List of Parameters):ReturnType;**
> > begin
> > > **statements**
> > end;

where **statements** must include at least one statement which assigns a value (that is, a *return value*) to the function's **name**.

The following program, CharFunc, contains a function called *tolower* which converts an upper case letter to lower case by adding 32 to its ASCII code. The function relies on the standard functions *chr* and *ord*. (See section on ordinal types for details.)

```
program CharFunc (input, output);
var
     letter : char;
function tolower(alpha : char) : char;
begin
     tolower : = chr(ord(alpha) + 32);
end;
begin    {Main body}
     writeln('Type in a capital letter');
     readln(letter);
     writeln('Its lower case is ',tolower(letter));
end.
```

If you run this program you should be aware that it will only operate correctly if an uppercase (capital) letter is input. (See the exercises at the end of this chapter.)

Procedures using Value Parameters

The earlier section on simple procedures contained a program called *SumUp*. That program included a procedure called *DrawaLine* which drew a line of 10 dashes. The program below, called LineDraw, includes a procedure *DrawaLine2* which allows dashed lines of any length to be drawn. This time, when we wish to call up the procedure *DrawaLine2*, we must specify how many dashes are to be drawn. This is achieved by writing *DrawaLine2(5)*, for example, which means draw a line of 5 dashes. Pascal must be informed that we will be calling the procedure DrawaLine2 with different values each time and so now when the procedure DrawaLine2 is declared the first line must be as follows:

```
procedure DrawaLine2 (Length : integer);.
```

This tells Pascal that *DrawaLine2* will be called with a value representing the length of the line to be drawn and that this value will be an integer; the identifier, *Length*, is an example of a *value parameter*. We say that we are calling the procedure DrawaLine2 with a value parameter.

The program below, called Linedraw, implements this procedure.

```
program LineDraw (input, output);
procedure DrawaLine2 (Length : integer);
var
    i : integer;
begin
    for i := 1 to Length do
        write('—'); {Write '—' the number of times specified by Length.}
    writeln;
end;
begin        {Main body.}
    DrawaLine2(5); { Calls procedure DrawaLine2 with the value 5 }
    DrawaLine2(29);{ Now calls DrawaLine2 with the value 29 }
    DrawaLine2(80);{ Now calls DrawaLine2 with the value 80 }
end.
```

As a further example of the use of value parameters, the program BoxOfStars is shown below. This program includes a procedure, *DrawBoxofStars*, which accepts two value parameters representing the number of rows and columns required for the box. For example, the procedure call

```
DrawBoxOfStars(5,20)
```

would produce the following box (5 by 20)

```
********************
*                  *
*                  *
*                  *
********************
```

```
program BoxOfStars (input, output);
const {Specify the printing characters}
    Star  = '*';
    Space = ' ';
procedure DrawBoxOfStars (Row, Column : integer);
var
    x, y : integer;
begin
    for x := 1 to Column do
        write(Star); {Produce the top row of stars.}
    writeln;
    for y := 1 to Row — 2 do {Put in the middle of the box.}
        begin
            write(Star);
```

```
            for x : = 1 to Column − 2 do
                write(Space);
                writeln(Star);
          end;
      for x : = 1 to Column do
          write(Star); {Produce the bottom row of stars.}
      writeln;
  end;
  begin                    {main body}
      DrawBoxOfStars(15,20); {Draw box of size 15 by 20.}
  end.
```

The format of a *procedure* using *value parameters* is

```
procedure name(ValueParameter List);
    begin
        statements
    end;
```

Procedures using Variable Parameters

There are times when we may require values to be *returned* from a procedure, rather like the way that a value is returned from a function. (See section on functions.) A function, however, returns one value only and sometimes we may require two or more values to be returned. Pascal allows us to use procedures with *variable parameters* in order to do this; the word *var* is used for this purpose. We begin by looking at a procedure which returns just one value in order to illustrate the idea.

The program is called DiceDouble and it contains the procedure *ThrowDie* which simulates the throwing of a single die by producing a random number in the range 1 to 6. The value on the die is produced in the same way as it was in the program DiceGame. (See the section on Miscellaneous Functions.) This time, however, we use a variable (*var*) parameter in our procedure so that after the procedure call has been executed, the value on the die will be returned by virtue of it being stored in the variable that we used when we called the procedure. The first line in our procedure declaration will be:

```
        procedure ThrowDie(var DieNumber : integer);
```

Note the position of the word *var*.

In the program we will call up the procedure *ThrowDie*, twice; the first time with the variable *Die1* and the second time with the variable *Die2*. The values returned into these variables will then be used to determine the total score and whether or not a double has been thrown.

```
    program DiceDouble (input, output);
    var
        x : integer;
        Total : integer;
        Die1, Die2 : integer;
    procedure ThrowDie(var DieNumber : integer);
```

```
begin
    DieNumber := random(6) + 1;
    write(' Throw is ', DieNumber);
end;
begin {Main body.}
    randomize;
    for x := 1 to 24 do {Write a screenful of die throws.}
        begin
            ThrowDie(Die1);
            ThrowDie(Die2);
            Total := Die1 + Die2;
            write(' Total is ', Total);
            if Die1 = Die2 then write(' A DOUBLE!!');
            writeln;
        end;
end.
```

The program *Dicedouble* has been rewritten below as *DiceDouble2* in order to show how to call up a procedure with two variable parameters. The procedure *ThrowDie* has been altered so that it now returns both the dice throws after being called just once.

```
program DiceDouble2 (input, output);
var
    x : integer;
    Total : integer;
    Die1, Die2 : integer;
procedure ThrowDie(var DieNo1, DieNo2 : integer); {Throws a pair of dice.}
begin
    DieNo1 := random(6) + 1;
    write(' Throw is ', DieNo1);
    DieNo2 := random(6) + 1;
    write(' Throw is ', DieNo2);
end;
begin {Main body.}
    randomize;
    for x := 1 to 24 do
        begin
            ThrowDie(Die1, Die2);
            Total := Die1 + Die2;
            write(' Total is ', Total);
            if Die1 = Die2 then write(' A DOUBLE!!');
            writeln;
        end;
```

end.

The format of a *procedure* using *variable parameters* is

```
procedure name(VariableParameter List);
    begin
        statements
    end;
```

User-Defined Data Types

In Pascal, the standard data types are *integer, real, char* and *boolean*. In addition, Pascal allows the programmer to declare his/her own data types. User-defined data types must be declared in a program, before any variables are declared, by using the word *type*. Hence, for any program, the structure will be as follows:

```
program name (input, output);
const
    {constant declarations go here}
type
    {type declarations go here}
var
    {variable declarations go here}
begin
    {main body of program}
end.
```

There are two kinds of *type* that can be declared; these are the *subrange type* and the *enumerated type*. There are two main reasons for using types; firstly, they can make programs more readable, and secondly, they help to validate data when it is entered into the computer.

Subrange Types

These allow the programmer to take an *ordinal* data type, such as *char* or *integer*, and specify a range of values associated with that data type. For example, suppose that we wish to declare a variable to store an employee number, which must consist of exactly four digits; the following declarations would suffice:

```
type
    FourDigitNo = 1000..9999;
var
    EmployeeNo : FourDigitNo;
```

Now, if say, a three digit number or a five digit number was read into the variable *EmployeeNo* this would cause the computer to detect incorrect data entry. Note that, depending upon the version of Pascal you are using, you may have to inform your compiler (by altering various settings) that you want it to check values as they are entered into subrange types. See your Pascal manual for details.

More examples of subrange type declarations are shown below:

```
type
      UpperCaseLetter : 'A'..'Z';
      LowerCaseLetter : 'a'..'z';
      Digit : 0..9;
      SummerMonth : 6..9;
      PositiveInteger : 1..maxint;
      Percentage : 0..100;
```

and examples of variables declared using some of these types are as follows:

```
var
      Capital, Initial : UpperCaseLetter;
      CountingNumber : PositiveInteger;
      SingleFigure : Digit;
      ExamMark : Percentage;
```

Enumerated Types

With an enumerated type, the programmer simply lists the values that the type will be allowed to take; the values are placed in round brackets. The examples below show how to declare some enumerated types.

```
type
      WeekDay = (Monday, Tuesday, Wednesday, Thursday, Friday);
      Weekend = (Saturday, Sunday);
      SummerMonth = (May, Jun, Jul, Aug, Sep);
      CatSpecies = (Manx, Chinchilla, Rex, Persian, Siamese, Abyssinian);
```

Variables based on these types could be:

```
var
      WorkingDay : WeekDay;
      RestingDay : Weekend;
      HolidayMonth : Summermonth;
      FelinePet : CatSpecies;
```

We can mix these two user-defined data types by basing a subrange type on an enumerated type; for example, assuming we have declared the type *WeekDay* as above, we could specify a type called *MidWeek* as follows:

```
type
      MidWeek : Tuesday..Thursday;
```

Pascal will infer from the previous declarations that *MidWeek* is a subrange of the type *WeekDay*.

Since enumerated types are by definition, ordinal types, they can be used with the ordinal functions *pred, succ* and *ord*. For example, given the type *Day*, declared as:

```
type
        Day = (Monday, Tuesday, Wednesday, Thursday, Friday, Saturday, Sunday);
```

then,

>   *succ(Tuesday)* is Wednesday,

>   *pred(Sunday)* is Saturday

and

>   *ord(Friday)* is 4.

Note that the first ordinal position is always 0; so therefore

>   *ord(Monday)* is 0.

Also, *pred(Monday)* and *succ(Sunday)* are undefined; care must be taken to avoid the predecessor of the first ordinal value and the successor of the last ordinal value in the enumerated set.

The use of enumerated types allows us to write loop statements such as:

```
for WeekDay : = Monday to Friday do
```

and

```
for SummerMonth : = Jun to Aug do
```

which aids readability considerably.

Input & Output with Enumerated Types

One problem with enumerated data types, however, is that they cannot be read and written directly using the normal reading and writing procedures (that is, *read, readln, write* and *writeln*). If these data types are used internally in a program this presents no difficulties, but if input or output is required then special procedures must be written to get around the problem. A good method to use for outputting the values stored in these data types is illustrated in the program below, called *PlayingCards*, which generates and outputs all of the 52 cards in a standard pack by the use of a nested loop.

```
program PlayingCards (input, output);
type
        CardSuit = (hearts, diamonds, spades, clubs);
        CardValue =(ace, two, three, four, five, six, seven, eight, nine, ten, jack,
        queen, king);
var
        x : integer;
        Suit : CardSuit;
        Card : CardValue;
procedure WriteSuit (S : CardSuit);
```

```
begin
    case S of
        hearts      : write('hearts ');
        diamonds    : write('diamonds ');
        spades      : write('spades ');
        clubs       : write('clubs ');
    end;
end;
procedure WriteCard (C : CardValue);
begin
    case C of
        ace         : write('ace ');
        two         : write('two ');
        three       : write('three ');
        four        : write('four ');
        five        : write('five ');
        six         : write('six ');
        seven       : write('seven ');
        eight       : write('eight ');
        nine        : write('nine ');
        ten         : write('ten ');
        jack        : write('jack ');
        queen       : write('queen ');
        king        : write('king ');
    end;
end;
begin {Main body.}
    x := 0;
    for Suit := hearts to clubs do
        for Card := ace to king do
            begin
                x := x + 1;
                WriteCard(Card);
                write('of ');
                WriteSuit(Suit);
                write(' ');
                if x mod 4 = 0 then
                    writeln;         {Start a new line after 4 cards}
                                     {have been written out.}
            end;
end.
```

The method employs a case statement in the procedures *WriteSuit* and *WriteCard*. *WriteSuit* writes out the value of a suit, and *WriteCard* writes out the value of a card. The case statement in each of these procedures matches each enumerated value to an equivalent *write* statement. Note the use of *value parameters* in these procedures.

Special routines must also be provided if we wish to enter data from outside the program into enumerated type variables. The program below, called *Humanoids*, demonstrates one way to accomplish this. The type *Humanoid* is defined as consisting of the values *man, woman, boy* and *girl*, and a variable named *Human* is declared as being of type *Humanoid*. The program is designed to assign a value to *Human* depending upon the user's input. The method is to read in the first character of the value ('m' for man, 'w' for woman etc.) into a character variable called *FirstLetter* and then use a case statement to map this letter into the appropriate value for *Human*. A *repeat..until* loop is used, along with the boolean variable *ValidLetter*, to make sure that the first letter read in is valid.

```
program Humanoids (input);
type
      Humanoid = (man, woman, boy, girl);
var
      Human : Humanoid;
      FirstLetter : char;
      ValidLetter : boolean;
begin
      repeat
            ValidLetter : = true;
            readln(FirstLetter);
            case FirstLetter of {Assign correct value to Human.}
                  'm'      : Human : = man;
                  'w'      : Human : = woman;
                  'b'      : Human : = boy;
                  'g'      : Human : = girl;
            else
                  ValidLetter : = false;
            end;
      until ValidLetter;
end.
```

Global and Local Variables

A *global* variable is one that can be used anywhere in a program. For the most part, the programs in this book use global variables; they are the variables that are declared at the beginning of a program before any procedures or functions are declared. A *local* variable, however, is one that is declared inside a procedure or function and can thus only be used inside that procedure or function. The parts of a program in which a variable can be used is called the *scope* of that variable. Thus, the scope of a global variable is the whole program.

In the program below, the variables *Letter* and *First* are global variables and can be used in the main body and in any procedure in the program (N.B. variable *First* is a special case, as explained below). The variables *Number*, *First* and *Second* are local to the procedure *Pretend1*. There is no confusion here regarding the scope of the variable *First* as far as the program is concerned; if *First* is referred to in procedure *Pretend1*, then the local variable *First*, will be the one used, if *First* is referred to in the main body of the program, or in the procedure *Pretend2*, then the global variable *First* will be used. Whatever happens to the local variable *First* will have no effect on the global variable *First* and vice-versa; as far as the compiler is concerned they are entirely different variables. Finally, the variables *Third* and *Fourth* are local to procedure *Pretend2* and so can only be used inside of *Pretend2*.

```
program GlobalAndLocal (input, output);
var            {Global variables.}
     Letter : char;
     First : integer;
procedure Pretend1 (var Number : integer);
               {Note: Number is local to Pretend1.}
var            {Local variables.}
     First : integer;
     Second : integer:
begin
  .
  .   {Processing statements here.}
  .
end;
procedure Pretend2
var {Local variables.}
     Third : real;
     Fourth : real
begin
  .
  .   {Processing statements here.}
  .
end;
begin          {Main body.}
  .
  .
end.
```

You may well wonder what the point of all this is. Well, local variables have certain advantages when compared with global variables:

(1) The same names can be given to independent variables declared in a number of different procedures and not be found confusing by the compiler; this means that for variables declared for common operations, such as loop control (for example, *x* or *counter*), and for storing temporary values (for

example, *temp*), we do not have to keep on inventing new names, or have to resort to such names as *x1*, *x2*, *x3* etc.

(2) Local variables save memory; a local variable is only created by the program when the procedure it is declared in is actually called up for execution, and it is destroyed when the procedure terminates. Global variables, on the other hand, stay resident in memory throughout the duration of the program. In situations where memory is limited, this may be an important factor.

(3) The use of local variables makes a procedure independent of the other parts of the program and provides the opportunity for re-using that procedure in other programs. This independence would not be possible if the procedure relied on global variables; when copied into another program those variables may well not exist, or, even worse, may conflict with existing variables. A good deal of program modification could be in order. Making procedures independent, or 'watertight', makes possible the provision of a library of procedures (or functions).

(4) By using local variables in procedures and functions we avoid having to unnecessarily alter the value of a global variable. Often, this does not matter, but situations can arise where a global variable has its value changed without the programmer being aware of it. The consequences can be far-reaching.

(5) When writing recursive functions and procedures, local variables and parameters are absolutely necessary. (See next section, on Recursion.)

Of course, there will be times when we require a procedure to communicate with other parts of a program. In this type of situation, communication is easily established by the use of *parameters*, as explained earlier.

Recursion

Many people have difficulty understanding the concept of recursion but it is really quite a simple idea. To put it concisely, to describe something recursively means to describe it in terms of itself. Within the context of functions and procedures, a function (or procedure) is said to be recursive if it makes a 'call' to itself. For example, a function called *ancestor* could contain, in its main body, a call to *ancestor*; this would make *ancestor* a recursive function.

The *factorial* of a number provides a good instance of recursion. A few examples should make the idea of a factorial clear. Note that only *whole* numbers are allowed to have factorials.

The factorial of 4 is calculated as follows:

$$4 \times 3 \times 2 \times 1$$

which equals 24.
The factorial of 5 is

$$5 \times 4 \times 3 \times 2 \times 1$$

which equals 120, and
the factorial of 6 is

$$6 \times 5 \times 4 \times 3 \times 2 \times 1$$

which equals 720.

Looking at the previous examples leads to a *recursive* definition of a factorial, which is as follows:

The factorial of any number can be obtained by multiplying that number by the factorial of the number that is one less than that number. Put in a more mathematical way, the factorial of a number *n* is equal to *n* multiplied by the factorial of *n* – *1*. For example,

the factorial of 6 = 6 × the factorial of 5

the factorial of 4 = 4 × the factorial of 3.

Here, we have described *factorial* in terms of itself; the word *factorial* is used in the description of what a factorial is. Some ideas can be expressed more easily using recursion, others cannot. Recursion can sometimes provide a simple, elegant solution to a programming problem. The program below, FactorialDemo illustrates how the factorial function can be programmed recursively.

```
program FactorialDemo (input, output);
var
      number : integer;
function factorial (fact : integer) : real;
begin
      if fact = 1 then
            factorial : = 1
      else
            factorial : = fact * factorial (fact – 1);{call up factorial recursively}
end;
begin          {main body of program}
      writeln('Enter a number between 1 and 20');
      readln(number);
      writeln('The factorial of ', number,' is ',factorial (number):1:0);
end.
```

Although only whole numbers are allowed to have factorials, the factorial procedure above returns a *real* value as its result. The reason for this is that the data type *integer* only allows numbers up to a maximum of 32767 to be stored and the factorials of even quite small numbers soon exceed this value. For instance, the factorial of 8 is 40320. (You could try using long integers (*longints*) if your version of Pascal supports them.)

A second example of a recursive function is given below in the program *PowersOfTen*, which rewrites powers of ten in longhand form (positive and 0 powers only), for example, 10^4 will be rewritten as 10000 by the function. The recursive function *TenToThePower* is very similar to the previous factorial function; to calculate the value of 10 raised to some power (or *exponent*) we can multiply 10 by the power of 10 raised to the power one less than before. For example:

$$10^6 = 10 \times 10^5$$

and

$$10^9 = 10 \times 10^8.$$

Taking 10^6 as an example, in programming terms this means calling up the function *TenToThePower* with a parameter whose value is 6 (representing the power) and then computing the result of multiplying 10 by the value returned by calling up the function with a parameter of 5. When *TenToThePower* is called with the parameter 5 it will have to multiply 10 by the value returned by calling up the function with a parameter of 4. This process will continue until there comes a point at which the function will not need to call itself again; this will happen when the function *TenToThePower* is called with a parameter whose value is 0 because the result *TenToThePower* will return is equal to 1. Its value is known and so there is no reason to perform any further recursion. At this point the actual computation of 10^6 can take place (none of the function calls have actually been completed yet); the program will work backwards through the function calls by completing each multiplication of 10 by the returned value from each recursive function call.

```
program PowersOfTen (input, output);

type
     PositivePower = 0..20;{Use subrange to keep powers within acceptable limits}

var
     Exponent : PositivePower;

function TenToThePower (Power : integer): real;

begin
     if Power = 0 then
          TenToThePower : = 1 {Statement needed to end the recursion.}
     else
          TenToThePower : = 10 * TenToThePower(Power — 1); {Recursive call.}
end;

begin
     write('Enter the power of 10 you require ');
     readln(Exponent);
     Writeln('Result is ',TenToThePower(Exponent):2:0);
end.
```

The two programs above illustrate the need for there to be some statement included in a recursive routine that will allow the recursion to end; without a statement of this kind recursion will occur forever, or, as is usually the case, the computer will run out of memory and the program will crash.

Furthermore, it should be noted that in each recursive call, some variable or other must be changed. In the above programs it was the value of the parameter that changed (by being decremented) with each successive call. Eventually, a parameter value was reached which halted further recursive calls.

Local Variables in Recursion

The program given below, called ReverseLine, relies upon a local variable when it makes its recursive calls. The program accepts a line of text and then writes it out in reverse order (that is, backwards). Remember, that the *scope* of a local variable is the procedure in which it is declared. When a procedure is called from within itself, Pascal creates a new local variable (or set of variables if required) for that call. If, for example, a procedure contained a local variable called *digit* then for each recursive call a new version of *digit* would be created, and all of these *digit* variables would be distinct.

In the program, Reverseline, each recursive call creates a new version of the local variable, *ch*, which is used to store the current character being input; however, as each character is entered, it cannot be output unless the *eoln* character is detected. This is because, if *eoln* is not detected, another recursive call is made in the program at a position prior to the statement which writes out the character stored in *ch*. Eventually, *eoln* will become true (because at some point the user will hit the ENTER key), and then all of the recursive calls will be completed. The computer will work backwards through the calls, from the last recursive call to the first, writing out the character stored in each local *ch* variable. Thus, the line of text will be reversed.

Without local variables, this form of recursion would not be possible.

```
program ReverseLine (input, output);
procedure WriteBackward;    {Recursive procedure}
var
     ch : char; {Declare local variable}
begin
     read(ch);
     if not eoln then
          WriteBackward {Make a recursive call to WriteBackward}
     else
          writeln; {Statement to terminate the recursion}
     write(ch);
end;
begin {Main body}
     writeln('Please enter a line of text to be reversed');
     writeln('Hit the ENTER key to finish');
     WriteBackward;
     writeln;
end.
```

Exercises

1   Do you think the game played by the program DiceGame is fair on the player or do you think the computer has an advantage? To see if you are right, modify DiceGame so that it plays around 500 games and counts how many times the computer wins and how many times the player wins. Run the program a few times until you are convinced about the fairness.

2   Modify the rules and the program for DiceGame so that the game is fairer. The player should win about 50% of the time.

3   Write a program which incorporates a function called *min* which will accept three real parameters and return the smallest one.

4   Modify the function *tolower* in program *CharFunc* so that it will only produce an output if an uppercase character is input. Use an *if..then* statement to check that the ordinal value of the character being input lies between 65 (which is 'A') and 90 (which is 'Z'). Prompt the user with a suitable message if incorrect input is attempted.

5   Write a program to print out part of the ASCII code set (or whichever code set your computer uses). Begin by printing out the codes 32 through to 127; this will avoid the ASCII control characters (0 to 31) which may play havoc with your program! Hint: Set up a loop running from 32 to 127 and use the ordinal function *chr* to print out the characters corresponding to each code. Once your program is running try writing out all of the codes from 0 through to 255.

6   Write a recursive function for the Fibonacci Series. This is the number series:

1, 1, 2, 3, 5, 8, 13, 21, 34, 55, 89, ...

where each number in the series, apart from the first two ones, is found by adding the previous two numbers together. For example, the 9th number in the series, 34, is found by adding together the 7th and 8th numbers in the series, namely 13 and 21.

Therefore, mathematically, the function can be written as:

$\text{Fibonacci}_1 = 1$, $\text{Fibonacci}_2 = 1$, and

$\text{Fibonacci}_n = \text{Fibonacci}_{n-2} + \text{Fibonacci}_{n-1}$ {where n > 2}

This provides enough information to write the Fibonacci function; note that the function requires two recursive calls in its main body.

7   Amend the PlayingCards program so that instead of the whole pack being displayed, a card is drawn from the pack at random.

The *random* function can be used to generate randomly a number between 0 and 3 to give an ordinal value for the suit, and a number between 0 and 12 for the ordinal value of a card in that suit. (Remember that the first ordinal value in any set is 0.)

As an enhancement, get your program to pick three cards at random. You must ensure, somehow, that the three cards are different.

Assignment

Write a program to play a dice game. The game can be as simple or as complicated as you wish to make it.

The nature and rules of the game are left entirely up to you; the game could be written, for example, for one, two or more players or for one player against the computer. The rules of the game could be invented by you or you could consider an existing game such as 'craps'.

Ambitious programmers may like to consider a game such as 'snakes and ladders' which requires a board to be drawn on-screen if it is to be effective. The graphics features of the version of Pascal to be used need to be investigated before embarking upon this type of game.

As usual, procedures (and functions) should be used.

Chapter 5

Files

Introduction to Files

There is often a need to store data permanently. The way to do this is to store the data in files which are held on magnetic disk (or tape). It is important to realize that everything stored on a disk will be held in a file of one sort or another. Even the Pascal programs you write are stored as files; each Pascal program is stored as a *text* file, which is just a file containing characters.

As with arrays, the components of a file must all be of the same type and, depending upon the type of file, the data in a file can be accessed either in *sequential* order or in *random* order. Accessing data in sequential order simply means starting at the beginning of a file and searching through it until the required data is reached. With random access, any part of a file can be accessed immediately, without having to carry out any searching. Obviously, random access is faster than sequential access. It should be noted that Standard Pascal does not support random access files.

Each file stored on disk must contain an *end-of-file* marker; this prevents a program from inadvertently reading in data from the next file stored on the disk. The treatment of files here assumes that the DOS operating system is being used. DOS uses the *ctrl-z* character as its end-of-file marker; the details of this will be supplied later. Detecting the beginning of a file is a task left up to the operating system and the details of how that is carried out need not concern the Pascal programmer.

As sequential files are supported by Standard Pascal, they will now be discussed at length. Random files will be introduced in a later section.

Text Files

Pascal contains a built-in file type called *text*. A text file is the simplest type of file available and can be visualized as containing characters written one after another along the length of the file. This type of file can only be accessed in sequential order.

Some new identifiers are needed in order to process files and these are:

> *assign   reset   rewrite*   and   *close.*

These will be explained as and when they are encountered in the programs which follow.

The first program, called TextWrite, stores characters in a text file as they are typed in at the keyboard. In order to terminate data entry, the user must enter *ctrl-z* (referred to as control z) which is achieved by holding down the *ctrl* key and then pressing the z key once. After z has been pressed, the *ctrl* key can be released.

```
program TextWrite (input, output);
var
    ch : char;
    txtfile : text;      {txtfile is a file of text}
begin
    assign(txtfile,'a:\txtfile.dat');
    rewrite(txtfile);
    while not eof do {terminate file with ctrl-z}
        begin
```

```
            read(ch);
            write(txtfile,ch);
        end;
    close(txtfile);
end.
```

Each character read from the keyboard (using *read* - see earlier section on this) will be held in a variable called *ch* until it is written to the file. The file is declared, in the *var* section of the program, as being a file of text called *txtfile*. In order to be stored on disk the file needs to be assigned an *external* file name. Inside the program (that is, in internal memory) the file is known as *txtfile* but the operating system needs to know the name that the file will be using when it is stored externally on disk. In this program, the internal file will be written to an external file called *txtfile.dat*, residing on a disk in drive *a:* of the computer. Hence the complete specification of the file is *'a:\txtfile.dat'* and the assignment operation is carried out by the statement:

```
assign(txtfile,'a:\txtfile.dat');.
```

Note the quotes around the external file name. If your computer does not use the DOS operating system please check your manual for details of file specifications.

The next statement is *rewrite(txtfile)*; which initializes *txtfile* and gets it ready to receive output from the computer, that is, it is ready to have data written to it. If *txtfile* contains any existing data, it will be lost. The main part of the processing is carried out by the while loop:

```
while not eof do
    begin
        read(ch);
        write(txtfile,ch);
    end;
```

which reads each character from the keyboard into *ch* and then writes it to the file using the statement

```
write(txtfile,ch);
```

This is the same *write* statement that we have used before for outputting data to the monitor, except that now we are requesting that the data be written to a file (by including the name, *txtfile*, in the statement) instead of to the monitor. Actually, the usual form of the *write* statement, as, for example, in the statement *write(ch);* is just a shorthand, more convenient way of writing out

```
write(output,ch);
```

which means write out *ch* to the standard output device, which is normally the monitor. Similarly, *writeln, read* and *readln* statements can be written out in full as, for example,

```
readln(input,ch);
```

which means read a character into *ch* from the standard input device, the keyboard. You should infer from all of this, that as far as DOS is concerned, the keyboard and monitor are treated in exactly the same way as files. In fact, DOS considers all input and output devices as being files.

The while loop is terminated when the end of the file, represented in Pascal by *eof*, is reached. The end of the file is detected by the user entering *ctrl-z*. As stated in the introduction, *ctrl-z* is DOS's standard end-of-file marker.

The condition for the loop to be executed is given as *not eof* (that is when *eof* is false) and so the condition for the loop to be terminated is when *eof* is true; in other words, the loop is terminated when the end of the (keyboard) file is reached.

Note that when the file is closed it will contain an end of file marker so that the next time it is read the end of the file can easily be detected. The file is closed by using the statement

```
close(txtfile);.
```

The next step is to write a program which will open up our file called *txtfile*, read it and print out its contents. The program is called *txtread* and is shown below.

```
program textread (input, output);
var
    ch : char;
    txtfile : text;      {txtfile is a file of text}
begin
    assign(txtfile,'a:\txtfile.dat');
    reset(txtfile);
    while not eof(txtfile) do {Note that txtfile must be specified here.}
        begin
            read(txtfile,ch);
            write(ch);
        end;
    close(txtfile);
end.
```

This program is virtually identical to *txtwrite*; the same variables are used and the *assign* statement is the same as before. This time, however, the file must be opened for reading rather than writing; this is achieved using the statement

```
reset(txtfile);
```

The same condition is used in the while loop as for writing, except that this time we must specify that the *eof* we are looking for is in the file called *txtfile* (hence the condition *not eof(txtfile)*). The data is read from the file using the statement

```
read(txtfile,ch);
```

which places each character, one at a time, into the variable *ch* so that it can be written to the monitor using the following statement

```
write(ch);
```

As before, the file is closed using the statement

```
close(txtfile);
```

It should be noted that, when dealing with sequential file access, a file can be opened for reading or writing but not both. Reading *and* writing to an opened file can only take place if the file can be randomly accessed (see later section on Random Access Files).

Files of Integers and Reals

Suppose we wish to store, in a file, some data relating to bank customers. The data to be stored in this case could consist of the customer's number (using the variable, *CustomerNumber*) and the balance (using the variable, *Balance*). This time, a file of text would not be appropriate; we need to store numbers. Numbers can be written using characters, of course, but if mathematical operations are to be carried out then the numbers must be stored as either integers or reals.

The components of a file must all be of the same type and so *CustomerNumber* and *Balance* are both declared as reals, and the file itself, *CustFile*, is declared as being a *file of real*. Declaring *CustomerNumber* and *Balance* as integers would be of no use, as balances, which consist of monetary amounts, normally involve decimal points. (We will see later how to store *records* which can contain data of different types.) Note that the external file name, *'a:\customer.dat'*, is assigned to the constant identifier, *FileName*, making it easier to refer to the external file in various parts of the program.

The program, called BankBalances, is given below.

```pascal
program BankBalances (input, output);
const
      FileName = 'a:\customer.dat';
var
CustFile : file of real; {Declare the file}
procedure CreateFile;
var
      x : integer;
      CustomerNumber, Balance : real;
begin
      writeln;
      writeln('You will be asked to enter data for 3 customers.');
      writeln('The data for each customer consists of an account');
      writeln('number (4 digits) and a balance (65.50 for example)');
      writeln;
      writeln('Press the ENTER key when you are ready');
      readln;
      assign(CustFile, FileName);
      rewrite(CustFile);
      for x := 1 to 3 do
            begin
                  writeln('Enter an account number');
                  readln(CustomerNumber);
                  writeln('Enter the balance for this account');
                  readln(Balance);
                  write(CustFile, CustomerNumber, Balance);
            end;
```

```
         close(CustFile);
end;
procedure ReadFile;
var
      x : integer;
      CustomerNumber, Balance : real;
begin
     writeln;
     writeln('Reading file from disk....' );
     writeln;
     assign(CustFile, FileName);
     reset(Custfile);
     while not eof (CustFile) do
          begin
               read(CustFile, CustomerNumber, Balance);
               writeln(CustomerNumber:6:0, Balance:8:2);
          end;
     close(CustFile);
     writeln;
end;
begin          {Main body}
     CreateFile;
     ReadFile;
end.
```

As you can see, the program creates the file of customers onto disk, closes the file, and then opens it up again to read the data and write it out onto the monitor. The program is very similar to the programs *txtread* and *txtwrite* except that this time the data is stored using real numbers. The procedures *CreateFile* and *ReadFile* use the same variable names (to avoid confusion) for writing and reading the data to and from disk but this need not necessarily be the case. Any variable names could be used as long as they were declared as being of type *real*.

As it stands, the program above does not do any worthwhile processing. A new version of *BankBalances*, which works out the total of all the individual balances, is given on the next page. The changes are as follows:

(1) The procedure *ReadFile* has been modified and renamed as *ProcessBalances*.

(2) *ProcessBalances* reads the data relating to each customer and adds each customer's balance to an overall balance called *TotalBalance*.

(3) After each customer's data has been written out, the total bank balance is displayed.

(4) The program has been renamed as *BankBalances2*.

```pascal
program BankBalances2(input, output);
const
    FileName = 'a:\customer.dat';
var
    CustFile : file of real;
procedure CreateFile;
var
    x : integer;
    CustomerNumber, Balance : real;
begin
    writeln;
    writeln('You will be asked to enter data for 3 customers.');
    writeln('The data for each customer consists of an account');
    writeln('number (4 digits) and a balance (65.50 for example)');
    writeln;
    writeln('Press the ENTER key when you are ready');
    readln;
    assign(CustFile, FileName);
    rewrite(CustFile);
    for x := 1 to 3 do
        begin
            writeln('Enter an account number');
            readln(CustomerNumber);
            writeln('Enter the balance for this account');
            readln(Balance);
            write(CustFile, CustomerNumber, Balance);
        end;
        close(CustFile);
end;
procedure ProcessBalances;
var
    x : integer;
    CustomerNumber, Balance, TotalBalance : real;
begin
    writeln;
    writeln('Reading file from disk....' );
    writeln;
    assign(CustFile, FileName);
    reset(Custfile);
    TotalBalance := 0;
    while not eof (CustFile) do {Loop until the end of Custfile is reached.}
```

```
            begin
                 read(CustFile, CustomerNumber, Balance);
                 TotalBalance : = TotalBalance + Balance;
                 writeln(CustomerNumber:6:0, Balance:8:2);
            end;
        close(CustFile);
        writeln;
        writeln('The total bank balance stands at ',TotalBalance:8:2);
    end;
    begin {main body}
        CreateFile;
        ProcessBalances;
    end.
```

Records

We have seen that an array variable can contain multiple values of a certain data type; for example the array *CustomerNumbers* could contain 30 integers representing 30 customer numbers. Remember that an array can only hold data of one specific type. There are, however, situations where we would like to have collections of data of differing types. For example, it is common for companies to store details of employees in a computer file, where each employee has his/her own record.

A simple record to be used for pay calculation purposes might consist of the employee's works number, name, hours worked and the hourly rate. Note that the data consists of different types, namely, integer, character string and two reals, respectively. The separate data items in the record are referred to as the *fields* of the record.

Pascal provides a special data structure for this, called, not surprisingly, the *record*. The way to declare a record of the type just discussed is shown below; each record to be used in the file consists of four *fields* and these have been given the names (or identifiers) *WorksNumber, Name, HoursWorked* and *HourlyRate*.

```
    type
        Entry =
            record
                WorksNumber : 1000..9999;
                Name : string[15];
                HoursWorked : real;
                HourlyRate : real;
            end;
```

Here, we haved declared the structure of a record of a certain *type* and we have given this record type the name, *Entry*. The fields of the record are placed between the words *record* and *end* and each field is named along with its own data type. A field can contain data of any type that Pascal recognizes. (Note that the *WorksNumber* field contains data of a sub-range type.)

The question now arises about how a collection of such records is organized as a file. The answer to this question is that the records are simply placed one after another in the file; remember, we are dealing with files that can only be accessed sequentially, not randomly. We can, if we wish, store our records in an array, so that we can easily set up loops for accessing the records in a file. This is the method we will adopt here; that is, we will declare an array of records for our file. The array, called *EntryList*, is declared by the statement

```
EntryList : array [1..3] of Entry;
```

which sets aside storage space for 3 records. We can, of course, have more records if required.

The program given below, called FileOfRecs, demonstrates these new ideas. Note that the file to be used by the program is called *PersonnelFile* and is declared as being a file of type *Entry*. Access to the individual fields of each record is facilitated by the use of the *dot notation*; for example, if we wished to refer to the field *WorksNumber* in record *EntryList[2]* we would write

```
EntryList[2].WorksNumber
```

and to refer to the field *HoursWorked* we would write

```
EntryList[2].HoursWorked.
```

In the program, a loop using the control variable, *x*, is used to identify and gain access to each record.

```
program FileOfRecs (input, output);
type
    Entry =
        record
            WorksNumber : 1000..9999;
            Name : string[15];
            HoursWorked : real;
            HourlyRate : real;
        end;
var
    EntryList : array [1..3] of Entry;
    x : integer;
    PersonnelFile : file of Entry;
procedure CreateFile;{Opens up the file and writes the data to it.}
begin
    assign(PersonnelFile,'a:\persnell.dat');      {External file is stored on}
                                                  {drive a: under the name persnell.dat.}
    rewrite(PersonnelFile);
    for x := 1 to 3 do
        begin{Prompt user for data for each record.}
            writeln;
            writeln('Enter data for record no. ',x);
            write('WorksNumber ');
            readln(Entrylist[x].WorksNumber);
```

```
                    write('Name ');
                    readln(Entrylist[x].Name);
                    write('HoursWorked ');
                    readln(EntryList[x].HoursWorked);
                    write('HourlyRate ');
                    readln(EntryList[x].HourlyRate)
                    write(PersonnelFile,EntryList[x]);   {Write the record to the file.}
                                                         {Dot notation unnecessary}
                                                         {for this operation.}
               end;
          close(PersonnelFile);
     end;
     procedure ReadFile;{Opens the file, reads the data and writes it to monitor.}
     begin
          assign(PersonnelFile,'a:\persnell.dat');
          reset(PersonnelFile);
          for x := 1 to 3 do
               begin
                    writeln;
                    writeln('Record No. ',x);
                    writeln;
                    read(PersonnelFile,EntryList[x]);{Read the record from the file.}
                    writeln('Works No. ',EntryList[x].WorksNumber);
                    writeln('Name ',EntryList[x].Name);
                    writeln('Hours Worked ',EntryList[x].HoursWorked:2:0);
                    writeln('Hourly Rate ',EntryList[x].HourlyRate:4:2);
               end;
          close(PersonnelFile);
     end;
     begin{Main body.}
          CreateFile;
          ReadFile;
     end.
```

The With..Do Statement

The above program used the dot (.) notation to access the individual fields in each record. That notation, however, makes programs look more complicated (and often uglier) than they should. Pascal provides a solution to this: the *with..do* statement, which allows the programmer to specify which record is to be manipulated and to then drop the record identifier in subsequent program instructions which involve that record. In the above program, this would mean that we would not need to write *EntryList[x]* every time we wanted to refer to a field in a particular record.

The following program, FileOfRecs2, demonstrates the use of the *with..do* statement.

```
program FileOfRecs2 (input, output);
type
    Entry =
        record
            WorksNumber : 1000..9999;
            Name : string[15];
            HoursWorked : real;
            HourlyRate : real;
        end;
var
    EntryList : array [1..3] of Entry;
    x : integer;
    PersonnelFile : file of Entry;
procedure CreateFile;
begin
    assign(PersonnelFile,'a:\persnell.dat');
    rewrite(PersonnelFile);
    for x := 1 to 3 do
        with EntryList[x] do{Specify which record to use.}
            begin
                writeln;
                writeln('Enter data for record no. ',x);
                write('WorksNumber ');
                readln(WorksNumber);
                write('Name ');
                readln(Name);
                write('HoursWorked ');
                readln(HoursWorked);
                write('HourlyRate ');
                readln(HourlyRate);
                write(PersonnelFile,EntryList[x]);
            end;{of with statement}
    close(PersonnelFile);
end;
procedure ReadFile;
begin
    assign(PersonnelFile,'a:\persnell.dat');
    reset(PersonnelFile);
```

```
        for x : = 1 to 3 do
            begin
                read(PersonnelFile,EntryList[x]);


                with EntryList[x] do
                    begin
                        writeln;
                        writeln('Record No. ',x);
                        writeln;
                        writeln('Works No. ',WorksNumber);
                        writeln('Name ',Name);
                        writeln('Hours Worked ',HoursWorked:2:0);
                        writeln('Hourly Rate ',HourlyRate:4:2);
                    end;
            end;
        close(PersonnelFile);
    end;
    begin {Main body.}
        CreateFile;
        ReadFile;
    end.
```

Note how the program is much easier to read and understand.

The format of the *with..do* statement is

```
with RecordIdentifier do
    begin
        statements
    end;
```

At the moment, our file handling program does not perform much in the way of processing; it just creates a file and then reads it. A natural use for the personnel file would be to calculate the amount of pay due to each employee (ignoring deductions such as tax, in order to keep the program simple). The procedure below, *CalculatePay*, which is written to replace the procedure *ReadFile*, will carry out this task.

```
procedure CalculatePay;
begin
    assign(PersonnelFile,'a:\persnell.dat');
    reset(PersonnelFile);
    for x : = 1 to 3 do
        begin
            read(PersonnelFile,EntryList[x]);
            with EntryList[x] do
```

```
                begin
                    writeln;
                    writeln('Works No. ',WorksNumber);
                    writeln('Name ',Name);
                    writeln('Hours Worked ',HoursWorked:2:0);
                    writeln('Hourly Rate ',HourlyRate:4:2);
                    Pay : = HoursWorked * HourlyRate;
                    writeln('Pay  =  ',Pay:4:2);
                end;
          end;
      close(PersonnelFile);
  end;
```

CalculatePay opens the file, reads in each record, calculates the pay using the statement

```
Pay : = HoursWorked * HourlyRate;
```

and then writes out the relevant data. Don't forget that the main body of the program should be changed to

```
begin {Main body.}
    CreateFile;
    CalculatePay;
end.
```

in order to run the program.

Updating Sequential Files

The method of updating a sequential file is as follows:

The file to be updated (that is, the *old* file) is opened for reading, along with a *new* file which is opened for writing. Data from the old file is read into the computer's memory, where it is updated in some way; the updated data items are then written to the new file. Note that a new file must be produced to hold the updated data; when dealing with sequential access it is not possible to open a file, amend it, and write the changes back to the same file.

The next program, called Employees, illustrates sequential file updating. Two files are used; these are named *Infile* and *Outfile*. Initially, *Infile* is created as the original (or *old*) file; *Outfile* will become the *new* file, to which the old file plus its updated items will be written. The files consists of records which contain an *EmployeeNumber* and a *PayToDate* field. This latter field is the one which is going to be updated.

The procedure, *CalculateNewPayToDate*, reads in each record from *Infile* and adds this week's pay, as entered by the user at run time into the variable *ThisWeeksPay*, to the current value of *PayToDate*. This produces an updated value of *PayToDate* for each record and this is written to the new file, *Outfile*, along with the appropriate employee number. Finally, a procedure called *CheckOutputFile* reads *Outfile* and writes its contents to the monitor so that the updated records can be inspected.

```
program Employees (input, output);
type
```

```
        Employee =
            record
                EmployeeNumber : integer;
                PayToDate : real;
            end;
    var
        Infile : array [1..3] of Employee;
        Outfile : array [1..3] of Employee;
        x : integer;
        InputFile : file of Employee;
        OutputFile : file of Employee;
        ThisWeeksPay : real;
    procedure CreateFile; {Creates the 'old' file which will be updated.}
    begin
        assign(InputFile,'a:\infile.dat');
        rewrite(InputFile);
        for x := 1 to 3 do {Just create 3 records for demonstration purposes.}
            with Infile[x] do {Enter the data onto the file.}
                begin
                    writeln;
                    writeln('Enter data for employee no. ',x);
                    write('EmployeeNumber ');
                    readln(EmployeeNumber);
                    write('PayToDate ');
                    readln(PayToDate);
                    write(InputFile,Infile[x]);
                end;
        close(InputFile);
    end;
    procedure CalculateNewPayToDate; {Updates the file.}
    begin
        assign(InputFile,'a:\infile.dat');
        assign(OutputFile,'a:\outfile.dat');
        reset(InputFile);
        rewrite(OutputFile); {Open both files, one for reading and one for writing.}
        for x := 1 to 3 do
            begin
                read(InputFile,InFile[x]);
                    with InFile[x] do
                        begin
                            writeln;
```

```
                          writeln('Works No. ',EmployeeNumber);
                          writeln;
                          writeln('Pay to date is ',PayToDate:4:2);
                          writeln;
                          writeln('Enter pay for this week ');
                          readln(ThisWeeksPay);
                          PayToDate : = PayToDate + ThisWeeksPay;
                          writeln('PayToDate now is ',PayToDate:4:2);
                          write(OutputFile,Infile[x]);
                    end;
          end;
     close(InputFile);
     close(OutputFile); {Close both files.}
end;
procedure CheckOutputFile;
begin
     assign(OutputFile,'a:\outfile.dat');
     reset(OutputFile);
     for x : = 1 to 3 do
          begin
               read(OutputFile,OutFile[x]);
                    with OutFile[x] do
                         begin
                              writeln;
                              writeln('Works No. ',EmployeeNumber);
                              writeln;
                              writeln('New pay to date is ',PayToDate:4:2);
                              writeln;
                         end;
          end;
     close(OutputFile);
     writeln('Press ENTER to continue ');
     readln;
end;
begin          {Main body.}
     CreateFile;
     CalculateNewPayToDate;
     CheckOutputFile;
end.
```

Note that, when this program has to be run again in order to enter the next week's pay, *Outfile* will have to be renamed as *Infile* and the original copy of *Infile* either renamed or destroyed.

Normally, two or three 'old' versions of a file are kept safe, just in case something should happen to the up-to-date file.

Random Access Files

Standard Pascal does not support random files but many versions of Pascal, such as Turbo Pascal, have made provision for this. Turbo Pascal, for example, uses a procedure called *seek* which can be used to access any record in a file by going directly to it without the need for any form of searching. *Seek* works like this: associated with any file is a variable called a *file pointer* which keeps track of the current position in the file; as the file is read, the file pointer advances along the file. If we consider a file of records, then at the beginning of the file, the file pointer will be pointing to the position in the file of the start of record number 0 (the first record in any file is numbered as zero); when this record is read, the file pointer will be pointing to the position of the start of the second record (that is, record number 1) and so on.

Seek allows the programmer to advance the file pointer to the start of any particular record in the file. Using *seek* allows the records in a file to be accessed *and* updated in random order. Note that *reset* should be used if a file is required to be updated.

The syntax of *seek* is:

seek(**filename, recordnumber**);

so, for example to access record number 5 (the sixth record) in a file called *ShipList* we would write:

seek(ShipList,5);

Seek cannot be used with text files.

The program below, called RandomFind, creates a file of five records (numbered 0 to 4) and includes a procedure called *FindRecord* which uses *seek* to locate records at random.

```
program RandomFind (input, output);
type
    Entry =
        record
            WorksNumber : 1000..9999;
            HourlyRate : real;
        end;
var
    X : integer;
    PersonnelFile : file of Entry;
    PersonalRecord : Entry;
    SelectedRecord : integer;  {Holds the number of the record requested by user.}
procedure CreateFile;          {Creates a file of records containing}
                               {works nos & hourly rates.}
begin
    assign(PersonnelFile,'a:\persnell.dat');
    rewrite(PersonnelFile);
    for X := 0 to 4 do
```

```
        begin
            writeln;
            writeln('Enter data for record no. ',X);
            write('WorksNumber ');
            readln(PersonalRecord.WorksNumber);
            write('HourlyRate ');
            readln(PersonalRecord.HourlyRate);
            write(PersonnelFile,PersonalRecord);
        end;
    close(PersonnelFile);
end;
procedure FindRecord; {Allows user to examine any record at random.}
begin
    assign(PersonnelFile,'a:\persnell.dat');
    reset(PersonnelFile);
    writeln;
    writeln('Which record do you require (0 – 4)?');
    write('Type in any other number to quit ');
    readln(SelectedRecord);
    while (SelectedRecord > = 0) and (SelectedRecord < = 4) do
        begin        {If record number between 0 and 4, locate required record.}
                     {otherwise quit loop.}
            seek(PersonnelFile,SelectedRecord); {Locate the start of reqd record}
            read(PersonnelFile,PersonalRecord); {and then read it.}
            with PersonalRecord do
                begin
                    writeln;
                    writeln('Works No. ',WorksNumber);
                    writeln('Hourly Rate ',HourlyRate:4:2);
                end;
            writeln;
            writeln('Which record do you require (0 – 4)?');
            write('Type in any other number to quit ');
            readln(SelectedRecord);
        end;
    close(PersonnelFile);
end;
begin        {Main body.}
    CreateFile;
    FindRecord;
end.
```

Updating Files Randomly

In the section on sequential files it was noted that a sequential file could only be updated by reading in each record, amending it, and then writing the updated records to a new file. Sequential files cannot be updated 'in place' but random files can.

The procedure *UpdateRecord*, shown on the next page, and which can be inserted into the previous program, does just that; the user can choose any record at random and then update it by changing the hourly rate. The changes will be made to the existing file; a new file is not required. Note that, when the required record has been found, read into memory, and the changes entered, *seek* must be used again before the record is written back to the file. The reason for this is that once the required record has been read, the file pointer will have advanced to the start of the next record; using *seek* again, with the same record number as before, ensures that the changes are written to the correct record. (Try omitting the second *seek* to see what happens.)

```
procedure UpDateRecord;
begin
     assign(PersonnelFile,'a:\persnell.dat');
     reset(PersonnelFile);
     writeln;
     writeln('Which record do you wish to update (0 — 4)?');
     write('Any other number to quit ');
     readln(SelectedRecord);
     while (SelectedRecord > = 0) and (SelectedRecord < = 4) do
         begin
             seek(PersonnelFile,SelectedRecord); {Locate required record.}
             read(PersonnelFile,PersonalRecord);
             writeln;
             writeln('Works No. ',PersonalRecord.WorksNumber);
             writeln('Hourly Rate ',PersonalRecord.HourlyRate:4:2);
             writeln;
             writeln('Enter the new hourly rate for this record ');
             readln(PersonalRecord.HourlyRate);   {Make the changes.}
             seek(PersonnelFile,SelectedRecord);  {Re-locate the start of record.}
             write(PersonnelFile,PersonalRecord); {Write the changes to record.}
             writeln;
             writeln('Which record do you require (0 — 4)?');
             write('Any other number to quit ');
             readln(SelectedRecord);
         end;
     close(PersonnelFile);
end;
```

The main body of the previous program should now be changed to:

```
begin        {Main body.}
    CreateFile;
    UpDateRecord;
    FindRecord; {To check the updates.}
end.
```

Exercises

1   Write a program which will list all of the ASCII characters along with their codes and then write them to a text file on disk. Write a program to read the file and write it out on the monitor.

2   Write a program to:

(a)   Allow a user to type in a paragraph of text and store it in a file on disk,

(b)   Read the file and write out the text that was entered with the difference that each sentence must be on a new line, with a blank line between each line.

For example, given the paragraph below:

At the beginning of the 1980's, the Japanese announced their intention to produce the next or fifth generation computers. These machines were to exhibit artificial intelligence and operate enormously faster than current machines. They were to be based on new priciples of operation and were to operate closer to the way that humans are thought to perform processing tasks.

The final output would be:

At the beginning of the 1980's, the Japanese announced their intention to produce the next or fifth generation computers.

These machines were to exhibit artificial intelligence and operate enormously faster than current machines.

They were to be based on new priciples of operation and were to operate closer to the way that humans are thought to perform processing tasks.

3   Extend the program called *Employees* so that it is more realistic. Increase the number of records in each file and the number of fields in each record.

Suggested new fields are:

Name, National Insurance Number, National Insurance Contributions to Date, Tax Code, Tax to Date, Tax Rate and Union Dues.

Add a new procedure, called *FindEmployee*, which will locate and display any particular record given the correct employee number. Non-existent employee numbers should cause an error message to be displayed to the user.

Assignment

Write a complete file-handling package for an application of your choice. You can use either sequential files or random files. (Remember that some versions of Pascal do not support random access files.)

Some typical applications are:

Medical/Hospital Records
Personnel/Payroll Files
Catalogues of Videos, Computer Games, Books, Music Cassettes/CD's, etc.
Student Records
Criminal Records
Supermarket Stock Control
Airline Flights

The processing operations available to the user should include:

Initial File Creation
Record Updating/Amendment
Record Insertion/Deletion
Information Retrieval - Locating individual records or sets of records matching some criterion (or criteria), for example, in a book catalogue, locating all books written by a particular author or produced by a particular publisher.

File/Record Print-Out.

Chapter 6

Advanced Topics

Apart from introducing a number of advanced programming techniques and data structures, this chapter contains a collection of rather longer, more complete programs, which serves to illustrate the way that programs should be structured in order to make them easier to read, write and modify.

Multi-Dimensional Arrays

The arrays that have been discussed so far have been one-dimensional; they have been merely lists of numbers, characters, records, etc., which we could visualize as single columns of data. Should we so desire, an array can have as many dimensions as we like. A *two-dimensional* array, that is, one with a certain 'height' and 'width', can be visualized as a table of data. When dealing with two-dimensional arrays it is usual to refer to the number of rows and columns that it has. For example, a two-dimensional array of integers having 5 rows and 4 columns could look like this:

	col 1	col 2	col 3	col 4
row 1	1123	222	56	109
row 2	9909	5455	8	5665
row 3	56	567	234	1000
row 4	2000	45	11	2001
row 5	156	100	111	23

and it would be referred to as a 5 by 4, (5 x 4) array, that is, one having a size of 5 x 4. Note that the order is always *row* then *column* when dealing with array size. Mathematicians often prefer to call arrays *matrices;* the above array would be referred to as a 5 x 4 *matrix.*

The individual items of data in the array, called the *elements* of the array, can each be identified and accessed by providing the appropriate row number and column number. For example, using the array above, and now giving it the name *NumberParcel*, we can identify the value *567* by noting that its position is row 3 and column 2. We can write this position as

    NumberParcel[3,2]

and therefore uniquely identify it. Thus, any element in *NumberParcel*, can be accessed or identified by writing:

    NumberParcel[Row,Column].

Examples of assignment statements using the array *NumberParcel* are shown below:

    X := NumberParcel[4,4];   {Copy element (4,4) into X}
    NumberParcel[5,4] := 0;   {Set element (5,4) to 0}
    NumberParcel[2,2] := NumberParcel[2,2] + 1;{Add 1 to element (2,2)}

and

```
        NumberParcel[1,2] : = NumberParcel[2,3];
        {Set element (1,2) to the same value as element (2,3)}
```

For the moment we are going to stick to two dimensions only and look at some demonstration programs. The first one is called *TwoDimArray* and it shows how to enter data into a two-dimensionl array and how to write it back out again. The array used in the program is called *TableOfNos* and is declared with the statement

```
    TableOfNos : array[1..RowSize,1..ColumnSize] of integer;
```

where *RowSize* and *ColumnSize* are the required number of rows and columns; at the moment 5 rows and 4 columns are specified using a *const* declaration.

Data is input to the array using a *for..to..do* statement which is executed 5 times, representing the number of rows (as given by *RowSize*), and which has another *for..to..do* loop nested inside of it. This latter loop is traversed 4 times for each row value, and represents the number of columns (as given by *ColumnSize*). The complete data entry routine is packaged together as a procedure called *EnterArrayData*. The same method is used for displaying the data once it has all been entered; the procedure for doing this is called *DisplayArray*.

```
    program TwoDimArray (input, output);
    const
        RowSize = 5;
        ColumnSize = 4; {Specify the size of the array}
    var
        Row, Column : integer;
        TableOfNos : array[1..RowSize,1..ColumnSize] of integer;
    procedure EnterArrayData;
    begin
        writeln;
        for Row : = 1 to RowSize do
            for Column : = 1 to ColumnSize do
                begin
                    write('Enter number for row ',Row,' and column ',Column,' ');
                    readln(TableOfNos[Row,Column]);
                end;
            writeln;
    end;
    procedure DisplayArray;
    begin
        writeln;
        writeln('Here is the data you entered');
        writeln;
        for Row : = 1 to RowSize do
            begin
                for Column : = 1 to ColumnSize do
```

```
                    write(TableOfNos[Row,Column]:8,' ');
              writeln; {Start a new line after each row.}
         end;
    writeln;
    writeln('Press ENTER to continue');
    readln;   {Hold the display until ENTER is pressed}
  end;
begin          {Main body of program}
    EnterArrayData;
    DisplayArray;
end.
```

The techniques described above are now applied to a realistic application; the data for a group of salesmen need to be stored in a file on disk. The program has to read in the sales data for 4 salesmen over a 6 week period. The data for each week consist of the number of sales that each salesman has made. After data entry, the user must be able to check that the data are correct before being stored onto disk. The table of data will look something like this:

	Week 1	Week 2	Week 3	Week 4	Week 5	Week 6
Salesman 1	34	22	33	3	33	3
Salesman 2	123	56	55	67	7	67
Salesman 3	67	100	67	67	56	66
Salesman 4	90	0	12	98	67	3

A two-dimensional array called *SalesTable* is used to store all of the sales data prior to it being written onto the disk. An array is appropriate because it will allow us to write straightforward procedures to display, examine and amend the sales data.

```
program SalesMen (input, output);
const
    NoOfSalesMen = 4;
    NoOfWeeks = 6;
    FileName = 'a:\Sales.dat';     {File will be stored on drive a:}
                                   {under the name 'Sales.dat'.}
var
    SalesMan, Week : integer;
    SalesTable : array[1..NoOfSalesMen,1..NoOfWeeks] of integer;
    SalesFile : file of integer;
procedure InputSalesData;
begin
    writeln;
    for SalesMan := 1 to NoOfSalesMen do
```

```
        for Week : = 1 to NoOfWeeks do
            begin
                write('Enter number of sales for Salesman ',SalesMan);
                write(' during Week ',Week,' ');
                readln(SalesTable[SalesMan,Week]);
            end;
        writeln;
end;
procedure ShowSalesData;
begin
    writeln;
    writeln('Here is the Sales data :-');
    writeln;
    write('        ');
    for Week : = 1 to NoOfWeeks do {Set up the headings for the weeks.}
        write('  Week ',Week:1);
    writeln;
    writeln;
    for SalesMan : = 1 to NoOfSalesMen do
        begin
            write('Salesman ',SalesMan);       {Display each salesman's number.}
            for Week : = 1 to NoOfWeeks do  {Display each salesman's data.}
                write(SalesTable[SalesMan,Week]:8,' ');
            writeln; {Start a new line for the next Salesman.}
        end;
    writeln;
    writeln('Press ENTER to continue');
    readln; {Hold the display until ENTER is pressed}
end;
procedure AmendSalesData;
                {Identifies data to be amended by requesting the row}
                {(given by Salesman) and column (given by Week) position}
                {of the incorrect data.}
var
    Reply : char;
begin
    writeln;
    write('Do you wish to amend any salesman''s data? ');
    readln(Reply);
    while (Reply = 'y') or (Reply = 'Y') do {Amend a data item.}
        begin
```

```
                    write('Enter the Salesman''s number ');
                    readln(SalesMan);
                    write('Enter the Week number ');
                    readln(Week);
                    write('Enter the new Sales value ');
                    readln(SalesTable[SalesMan,Week]);
                    ShowSalesData; {Display the table.}
                    write('Do you wish to amend any more sales data? ');
                    readln(Reply);
              end;
     end;
     procedure WriteSalesDataToDisk;
                    {Uses a sequential file to store the sales data onto disk.}
     begin
          assign(SalesFile, FileName);
          rewrite(SalesFile);
          writeln;
          writeln('Writing data to disk ..... ');
          writeln;
          for SalesMan : = 1 to NoOfSalesMen do
               for Week : = 1 to NoOfWeeks do
                    write(SalesFile, SalesTable[SalesMan,Week]);
          close(SalesFile);
          writeln('Data file written');
          writeln;
          write('Press ENTER to quit the program ');
          readln;
     end;
     begin {Main body of program.}
          InputSalesData;
          ShowSalesData;
          AmendSalesData;
          WriteSalesDataToDisk;
     end.
```

Arrays in 3 Dimensions

Finally, we come to the three-dimensional array (or *3-D array*) which we can visualize as a *set* of two-dimensional tables. Using the *Salesmen* program as an example, suppose that we require tables of sales data as before, but now there is to be a table for each of three products sold by the salesmen.

The format of the data will look like this:

Product 1

	Week 1	Week 2	Week 3	Week 4	Week 5	Week 6
Salesman 1	34	22	33	3	33	3
Salesman 2	123	56	55	67	7	67
Salesman 3	67	100	67	67	56	66
Salesman 4	90	0	12	98	67	3

Product 2

	Week 1	Week 2	Week 3	Week 4	Week 5	Week 6
Salesman 1	341	122	3	123	53	45
Salesman 2	12	6	5	167	65	7
Salesman 3	7	10	101	67	96	36
Salesman 4	91	20	112	8	7	54

Product 3

	Week 1	Week 2	Week 3	Week 4	Week 5	Week 6
Salesman 1	14	52	73	23	63	11
Salesman 2	173	16	25	57	22	67
Salesman 3	68	103	68	47	56	96
Salesman 4	93	20	82	78	5	9

The program below, called SalesMen2 shows how to declare a 3-D array, enter data into the array (procedure *InputSalesData*) and then write it out again (procedure *ShowSalesData*). The only real difference in processing, between a 3-D array and a 2-D array, is that three loops are required in the nesting instead of the previous two. Thus, an extra outer loop has been added to provide a separate table for each product.

```
program SalesMen2 (input, output);
const
    NoOfSalesMen = 3;
    NoOfWeeks = 4;
    NoOfProducts = 3;
var
    SalesMan, Week, Product : integer;
    SalesTable : array[1..NoOfProducts,1..NoOfSalesMen,1..NoOfWeeks] of
    integer;
                             {Declare SalesTable as a 3-D array.}
procedure InputSalesData;
begin
```

```
     writeln;
     for Product : = 1 to NoOfProducts do
          for SalesMan : = 1 to NoOfSalesMen do
               for Week : = 1 to NoOfWeeks do
                    begin
                         write('Enter number of sales for Salesman ',SalesMan);
                         write(' during Week ',Week,' for Product ',Product,' ');
                         readln(SalesTable[Product,SalesMan,Week]);
                    end;
          writeln;
end;
procedure ShowSalesData;
begin
     writeln;
     writeln('Here is the Sales data :–');
     writeln;
     for Product : = 1 to NoOfProducts do
          begin
               writeln('Product No. ',Product);
               writeln;
               write('          ');
               for Week : = 1 to NoOfWeeks do
                    write('  Week ',Week:1);
               writeln;
               writeln;
               for SalesMan : = 1 to NoOfSalesMen do
                    begin
                         write('Salesman ',SalesMan);
                         for Week : = 1 to NoOfWeeks do {Innermost loop.}
                              write(SalesTable[Product,SalesMan,Week]:8,' ');
                         writeln;          {Start a new line after each Salesman.}
                    end;          {End of (middle) SalesMan loop.}
               writeln;
          end; {End of outer (Product) loop.}
     writeln;
     writeln('Press ENTER to continue');
     readln;                    {Hold the display until ENTER is pressed}
end;
begin          {Main body of program.}
     InputSalesData;
     ShowSalesData;
end.
```

Arrays of four dimensions or more are possible but are not considered here.

Fast Sorting Techniques

The *BubbleSort* was described in chapter 3 and, whilst it is suitable for sorting small amounts of data, it is hopelessly slow when dealing with large amounts of data (1000 or more items). Two faster methods of sorting that are available are the *ShellSort* and the *QuickSort*, of which the *QuickSort*, as would naturally be assumed, is the fastest.

Although the two programs below sort integers into order it should be noted that other data types and data structures, such as reals, character strings, or records, can all be sorted using the same techniques. The programs provided are written in Standard Pascal, except for the use of a random number generating function (*random*) to produce 1000 numbers.

A brief description of each sort is provided; the finer details of the workings of each sort can be found in the program annotation.

The ShellSort

This method of sorting divides the array of numbers into groups which can then be sorted separately. For example, suppose the array contained 16 numbers to be sorted; those data items which were 8 positions apart (that is, where there was a *gap* of 8 between the items) would be sorted first. There would be 8 groups, each one containing 2 items to be sorted. The next step would be to half the gap, thereby reducing it to 4; there would now be 4 groups, each group containing 4 items to be sorted. Halving the gap to 2 would produce 2 groups, each containing 8 items to be sorted. Finally, the gap would be halved to a distance of 1.

The success of the ShellSort lies in its ability to discover, early on in the sort, those items that are wildly out of position. Later passes thus require very few movements of data. A program to implement this method is shown below.

```
program ShellSort (output);
const
      NumberOfItems = 1000;
var
      M :array[1..NumberOfItems] of integer;
      I, Gap, Pnt1, Pnt2, Pnt3, Pnt4, Temp :integer;
procedure Exchange;
begin
      Temp := M[Pnt1];                               {swap keys using temporary}
      M[Pnt1] := M[Pnt2];                            {location}
      M[Pnt2] := Temp;
      Pnt4 := Pnt1;                                  {set pointers for pass}
      Pnt3 := Pnt1 – Gap;
      while (Pnt3>0) and (M[Pnt3] > M[Pnt4] do       {not top of list and}
          begin                                      {swap needed}
              Temp := M[Pnt3];                       {swap keys using temporary}
              M[Pnt3] := M[Pnt4];                    {location}
```

```
          M[Pnt4] : = Temp;
          Pnt3 : = Pnt3 - Gap;                    {move pointers up the list}
          Pnt4 : = Pnt4 - Gap;
      end;
  end;
procedure Sort;
begin
    Gap : = NumberOfItems;                        {At start set gap to full list}
    repeat
        Pnt1 : = 1;                               {set pointer to top of list}
        Gap : = trunc(Gap/2);                     {calculate gap between keys}
        Pnt2 : = Pnt1 + Gap;                      {set pointer to second key}
        repeat
            if M[Pnt1] > M[Pnt2] then             {compare keys, if wrong order}
                Exchange;                         {execute procedure exchange}
                Pnt1 : = Pnt1 + 1;                {move pointers down the list}
                Pnt2 : = Pnt2 + 1;
            until Pnt2 > NumberOfItems;           {test for bottom of list}
    until Gap = 1;                                {sort completed}
end;
begin           {Main body of program.}
    write('Creating ',NumberOfItems,' random numbers...');
    randomize;
    for I : = 1 to NumberOfItems do
        M[I] : = Random(30000);
    writeln;
    write('Sorting  ',NumberOfItems,' random numbers...');
    Sort;                                         {call sort procedure}
    writeln;
    for I : = 1 to NumberOfItems do
        write(M[I]:8);
                                                  {display sorted array}
    writeln;
    writeln('Hit the ENTER key to continue');
    readln;
end.
```

The QuickSort

This type of sort initially divides the array of numbers into two partitions centred on the mid-point of the array. The data items in the partition to the left of the mid-point are then compared, (starting at the far left of the partition), to the mid-point value until an item is found that is greater than or equal to the mid-point value; the data items in the right hand partition, (starting at the far right of the partition), are similarly compared with the mid-point value until an item is found that is less than or equal to the mid-point value. The two items are then swapped over. This process continues until all the items in each partition have been compared with the mid-point value and swapped, where necessary.

The same method is then applied (recursively) to the left and right partitions until every partition contains only one data item; at this point the array is completely sorted. The underlying principle involved here is that swaps should preferably be made between items that are positioned a great distance apart in the array. A QuickSort demonstration program is given below.

```
program QuickSort(output);
const
     NumberOfItems = 1000;
var
     M :array[1..NumberOfItems] of integer;
     I, Low, High :integer;
procedure Sort(var LowEnd, TopEnd :integer);
var
     LeftPntr, RightPntr, MidValue, Temp :integer;
begin
     LeftPntr : = LowEnd;                        {set pointers to current left}
     RightPntr : = TopEnd;                       {and right partition limits}
     MidValue : = M[(LowEnd + TopEnd) div 2];{store value at midpoint}
                                                 {between new left and right}
                                                 {partitions}

     repeat
         while M[LeftPntr] < MidValue do         {continue pass of left partition}
             LeftPntr : = LeftPntr + 1;          {while mid val greater than each}
                                                 {key examined}

         while MidValue < M[RightPntr] do        {continue pass of right partition}
             RightPntr : = RightPntr - 1;        {while mid value less than each}
                                                 {key examined}

             if LeftPntr < = RightPntr then{if pointers have not yet}
                 begin                           {crossed, swap the smaller key in the}
                                                 {right partition with the larger key}
                                                 {in left partition}

                     Temp : = M[LeftPntr];
                     M[LeftPntr] : = M[RightPntr];
                     M[RightPntr] : = Temp;
                     LeftPntr : = LeftPntr + 1; {move lpointer one right}
                     RightPntr : = RightPntr - 1;{move rpointer one left}
                 end;
```

```
            until LeftPntr > RightPntr;              {until pointers cross}
            if LowEnd < RightPntr then               {if left partition has more than}
                Sort(LowEnd, RightPntr);             {one element proc calls itself}
                                                     {to sort left partition with new}
                                                     {parameters}

            if LeftPntr < TopEnd then                {if right partition still has more}
                Sort(LeftPntr, TopEnd);              {than one element, proc calls}
                                                     {itself with new parameters}
        end;
        begin         {Main body of program.}
            write('Creating ',NumberOfItems,' random numbers...');
            {fill array with random numbers}
            randomize;
            for I: = 1 to NumberOfItems do
                M[I]: = Random(30000);
            writeln;
            write('Sorting ',NumberOfItems,' random numbers...');
            Low : = 1;                               {initialize lower and upper limits}
            High : = NumberOfItems;                  {of array}
            Sort(Low, High);                         {call recursive quicksort procedure}
            writeln;
            for I: = 1 to NumberOfItems do
                write(M[I]:8);                       {display sorted array}
            writeln;
            writeln('Hit the ENTER key to continue');
            readln;
        end.
```

Searching Techniques

In computing, the term *searching* means the process of locating some data item or items that are stored in the computer's memory. Often, the data to be located may be stored *externally* (that is, outside of computer memory); in this case the data will be stored in a file residing on some form of magnetic disk or tape. Before the required data can be searched for it must be copied from the disk into the computer's memory. (See section on files.) The treament given below assumes that the data is already in computer memory and that it is stored in an array; the methods considered are the *linear search*, the *binary search* and *hashing*.

The Linear Search

The simplest form of search is the *linear* or *sequential search*, where data items are examined one after another, in the order in which they were stored, until the required item is found. A program to carry out a linear search really just consists of a loop which is traversed as many times as there are data items, and a statement which compares each data item with the item to be found. Once found, the position of the item is stored so that it can subsequently be used.

The linear search can be speeded up somewhat by exiting the loop once the required data item is found. The program below, called StolenCards1, uses this method.

StolenCards1 is designed to establish whether or not a given credit card number (*CardNumber*) is in a list (*CardList*) which stores the numbers of stolen credit cards.

```
program StolenCards1 (input, output);
const
      Size = 12; {Gives the number of cards in the list.}
var
      CardNumber : integer; {Stores the card number to be searched for.}
      CardFound : boolean;
      CardList : array[1..Size] of integer;
      Position : integer; {Keeps track of current position in the list.}
procedure Initialize;
begin
      CardFound := false;
      CardList[1] := 1234; CardList[2] := 2123; CardList[3] := 3123;
      CardList[4] := 4123; CardList[5] := 5123; CardList[6] := 6123;
      CardList[7] := 7123; CardList[8] := 8123; CardList[9] := 9123;
      CardList[10]:=10123; CardList[11] := 11123; CardList[12] := 12123;
end;
procedure Search;
begin
      write('Enter card number – up to 5 Digits only please! ');
      readln(CardNumber);
      Position := 1;
      repeat
          if CardList[Position] = CardNumber then
              CardFound := true {Record that the card has been found.}
          else Position := Position + 1;
      until (CardFound or (Position > Size));
      if CardFound then
          writeln('Stolen card is located in position ',Position)
      else
          writeln('That card is not in the stolen list')
end;
begin {main body of program.}
      Initialize;
      Search;
end.
```

The procedure *Initialize* uses assignment statements (for convenience) to set up an array of 12 (the value in *Size*) stolen cards. Any size of card list can be set up by changing the value of the constant *Size*.

The statement

```
if CardList[Position]  =  CardNumber then
     CardFound : =  true
```

checks to see if the data at the current position in *CardList* is the data that is being searched for. If it is, then the boolean variable *CardFound* is set to the value *true* and this causes immediate exit from the loop. The stolen card numbers are stored in numerical order but they don't have to be, as the search will examine every data item in the list until either the required card number is found or the end of the list is reached.

The conditions for loop termination are thus *CardFound* or *(Position > Size)*. The search starts at position 1 in the list and progresses through the list, one item at a time, by incrementing the variable *Position*; this is carried out by the statement *Position := Position + 1*, which is executed each time the condition *CardList[Position]* = *CardNumber* is found to be false. Finally, depending upon the value of *CardFound*, either the position of the stolen card is displayed or the user is informed that the card number is not in the list of stolen cards.

The Binary Search

The linear search is adequate for small amounts of data; the speed of the computer masks the amount of searching which takes place. For large amounts of data, however, the linear search is far too time-consuming. For example, in a list of one million items, about half a million items, on average, will need to be examined before the required item is found. The binary search, on the other hand, will only need to examine 20 items *at most* in order to find the required item of data in a list of this size. This represents an incredible saving in time.

The idea behind the binary search is very simple. For this description assume that the data consists of numbers. The data is first sorted into order using one of the standard sorting techniques, and then the binary search starts off by going to the middle of the sorted list, that is, it first locates the mid-point. At this stage the data item found is compared with the data item that is required. If the two items match then the required item has been located. If the item found is the larger of the two (in numerical terms) then the required item must reside in the top half of the sorted list (that is, between the first item and the middle item); if the item found is the smaller of the two then the required item must reside in the bottom half of the sorted list (that is, between the middle item and the last item).

At this point, half of the list can be discarded because it is now known in which half of the list the required item lies. The search now moves to the middle of the half of the list in which the required item lies and the whole process described above is carried out again. This is repeated until either the required item is found or it is established that the item is not in the list.

The binary search thus works by systematically halving the list each time a piece of data has been found and examined; hence the name binary search or binary chop. A short calculation should convince you that only 20 halving operations are required, at most, to get down to the one item that is required in a list of 1,000,000 data items:

1,000,000	halved produces		500,000
500,000	''	''	250,000
250,000	''	''	125,000
125,000	''	''	62,500
62,500	''	''	31,250
31,250	''	''	15,625
15,625	''	''	7,813 {Round up to get rid of fractions}
7,813	''	''	3,907
3,907	''	''	1,954
1,954	''	''	977
977	''	''	489
489	''	''	245
245	''	''	123
123	''	''	62
62	''	''	31
31	''	''	16
16	''	''	8
8	''	''	4
4	''	''	2
2	halved produces		1 {20 halving operations}

The program which follows, called StolenCards2, uses a binary search to establish whether or not a given credit card number (*CardNumber*) is in a list (*CardList*) which stores the numbers of the stolen cards.

```
program StolenCards2 (input, output);
const
     Size = 12;
var
     low, high, mid, CardNumber : integer;
     CardFound : boolean;
     CardList : array[1..Size] of integer;
procedure initialize;
begin
     low := 1;
     high := Size;
     CardFound := false;
```

```
        CardList[1] : = 1234; CardList[2] : = 2123; CardList[3] : = 3123;
        CardList[4] : = 4123; CardList[5] : = 5123; CardList[6] : = 6123;
        CardList[7] : = 7123; CardList[8] : = 8123; CardList[9] : = 9123;
        CardList[10]: = 10123;  CardList[11]  : = 11123;  CardList[12]  : = 12123;
    end;
    procedure BinarySearch;
    begin
        writeln('Enter card number — Digits only please!');
        readln(CardNumber);
        while (low < = high) and not (CardFound) do
            begin
                mid : = (low + high) div 2;
                if CardList[mid] = CardNumber then
                    CardFound : = true;
                if CardList[mid] > CardNumber then
                    high : = mid — 1;
                if CardList[mid] < CardNumber then
                    low : = mid + 1;
            end;{while}
                if CardFound then
                    writeln('Stolen card is located in position ',mid)
                else
                    writeln('That card is not in the stolen list')
    end;
    begin {main body of program}
        initialize;
        BinarySearch;
    end.
```

As in the program *StolenCards1*, the list of stolen cards is limited to 12 (set by the constant *Size*), and the stolen card numbers are allocated to the stolen card list using assignment statements - see the procedure *initialize* - which place the card numbers in correct numerical order. In an actual application of this kind the sorted set of stolen card numbers would probably be held in a file on disk and read into the program as and when required.

The variables *low*, *high* and *mid* each store, respectively, the position of the lowest card number, the position of the highest card number and the position of the middle card number, in the portion of the list to be currently searched. The variables *low* and *high* are initially set to the values 1 and *Size* (that is, 12) respectively so that at the outset the entire list of cards will be the portion that is required to be searched. A boolean variable, *CardFound*, is used to indicate whether or not the required card number has been found; initially this variable is set to the value *false*.

The procedure which does the actual searching, *BinarySearch*, operates as follows. The user types in a card number and a *while* loop is then entered. The first statement in this loop

      mid : = (low + high) div 2;

computes the position of the middle of the list and stores it in *mid*. The card number residing in the list in the position given by *mid* is then compared with the card number entered by the user (stored in *CardNumber*) by the following statements:

    if CardList[mid] = CardNumber then   {first *if* condition}
        CardFound : = true;
    if CardList[mid] > CardNumber then   {second *if* condition}
        high : = mid − 1;
    if CardList[mid] < CardNumber then   {third *if* condition}
        low : = mid + 1;.

If the first *if* condition is true then the card number is in the list and this is indicated by setting *CardFound* to the value *true*. The required card number will be in the position pointed to by *mid*. If the second *if* condition is true this means that the first half of the list must now be searched; thus *high* is set to the current mid-point of the list and 1 is subtracted so that the mid value will be ignored during the next search. (The number at *mid* was not the number that we were looking for, so why bother including it in the next search?) If the third *if* condition is true this means that the second half of the list must now be searched; thus *low* is set to the current mid-point of the list and 1 is added so that the mid value will be ignored during the next search.

If the card number was not found during the first execution of the *while* loop then the loop will be executed again but this time the value of *mid* will be half way between the start and middle of the list or half way between the middle and end of the list; exactly which half will depend on the card number that was input.

The loop will be executed repeatedly until either the card number is found in the list or it is apparent that it is not in the list. The conditions for loop termination are

      (low < = high) and not (CardFound).

The second condition *not (CardFound)*, will cause the loop to terminate when the card number is found; if *CardFound* is true then *not CardFound* must be false and so the complete *while* condition must also be false. (If two conditions are *'and'ed* together they must both be true in order for a *while* loop to be executed.) The first condition (*low* < = *high*) may not be so obvious. As the portion of the list to be searched gets smaller and smaller there will be a point at which the values of *low* and *high* will become equal; in other words the portion of the list to be searched has been reduced to only one card number. If this card number is not the required one then the next value of *low* or *high* to be computed (by adding 1 to *low* or subtracting 1 from *high)* will cause *low* to become greater than *high*. If this happens then the card number searched for cannot possibly be in the stolen list and so the search should be aborted. Finally, the result of the search, based on the value *of CardFound*, is output.

Hash Tables

Hash tables are an attempt to eliminate, as far as possible, any actual searching for data. The method tries to locate the required data item at the *first attempt* by *calculating* the position of that item in the hash table.

The method operates as follows. The hash table is initially empty. The position or *address* of any data item to be inserted into the hash table is calculated by a suitable formula; this formula or *hashing algorithm* will be based upon the nature of the data, the size of the table etc. and may be very simple or extremely complicated. We will content ourselves with simple hashing algorithms. When the time comes to locate a data item in the table, the same hashing algorithm is used to calculate its position.

There are, however, problems associated with this method. The first problem is that two or more data items may produce the same address when the formula is applied. One simple solution to this problem is to examine the contents of the address that has been produced by the formula and see if it is empty; if it is empty then the data can be stored at that address, but if not, then the next free location down the list can be used. This will obviously force some amount of searching to be carried out, but a good hashing algorithm will try to avoid too many data items producing the same address.

The second problem which is likely to occur is that some data item may produce an occupied address, and when an empty location is looked for further down the table, the end of the table is reached before a suitable location is found. One answer to this is to go back to the beginning (the top, that is) of the table and to seek an empty location from there downwards. A location will eventually be found because the size of the table must always be chosen to be larger than or equal to the number of items to be stored in the table.

One final point to note is that, in practice, hash tables are rarely filled to capacity. This is because, as a table gets filled up, there is less and less likelihood of a new data item finding an empty location at the first attempt. As more and more items have to search for empty locations, the 'knock-on effect' makes finding an empty location increasingly time-consuming. Thus, the subsequent searching for data in the table, which, remember, uses the same formula as for storing the data, takes longer and longer. This defeats the object of using the hash table in the first place, which was to try and avoid searching. Normally, hash tables are filled to between 50% and 75% of their full capacity.

The accompanying program, called HashTable, sets up an empty table and then invites the user to enter data into the table. A procedure called *EmptyTheTable* resets the table so that every location in the table is set to the value −1. This value of −1 is used later in the program to detect whether or not a location is empty.

The user can have a table of any required size by altering the value of the constant, *TableSize*. The actual number of values to be inserted into the table is stored in the variable, *Count*; the user is asked to type in the number of values that will be hashed into the table. Each data item should consist of a maximum of 4 digits. As data items are entered they are held, temporarily, in the variable, *DataItem*.

The process of placing the data items into their correct positions is carried out by the procedure, *CreateTable*. The address (or position) of each data item in the table is initially calculated by the simple hashing formula:

```
TablePos : = DataItem mod TableSize;
```

which merely gives *TablePos* the value of the remainder after dividing the value in *DataItem* by the value in *TableSize*. For example, if *TableSize* is 10 then the data item having the value 1234 will be stored in position 4, because 1234 divided by 10 is 123 with a remainder (or *mod*) of 4. (See section on integer division.)

The next step is to check the location to see if it is empty, in other words 'does it contain the value –1?' If it does then the data item is stored at that position; if it doesn't then the program will have to move forward through the table seeking out the next free location. This is accomplished using procedure *CheckForEmptyLoc*. If the bottom of the table is reached and still no empty location has been found then the program goes to the start of the table and seeks out an empty location from that point, once again by using *CheckForEmptyLoc*. Note the use of the boolean variable *FoundEmptyLoc* to indicate that an empty location has been found.

When all data items have been entered into the table, the table is written out using the procedure, *DisplayTable*, so that it can be inspected. The procedures *FindDataItem* and *CheckIfFound* carry out the task of searching for a requested data item. Basically, they operate in the same manner as *CreateTable* in the way that the table is worked through in search of an item. The difference is that each item found in the list must be compared with the item that has been requested. If the requested item is located then the boolean variable *ItemFound* is set to *true* and the position of the located item is copied into *FoundPos*. When the search is complete, the values stored in these two variables are used to issue a suitable message to the user regarding whether or not the item has been found; if it has been found, its position is displayed.

```
program HashTable (input, output);
const
    TableSize = 10;
var
    Table : array[1..TableSize] of integer;
    x : integer;
    Count : integer;
    DataItem : integer;
    TablePos : integer;
    FoundEmptyLoc : boolean;
    {The variables below are used when locating an item in the table.}
    ItemToBeFound : integer;
    FoundPos : integer;
    ItemFound : boolean;
procedure DisplayTable;
begin
    writeln;
    writeln('Position   Data Item');
    for x : = 1 to TableSize do
```

```
            writeln(x : 8, Table[x] : 12);
        writeln;
    end;
    procedure EmptyTheTable;
    begin
        for x := 1 to TableSize do
            Table[x] := -1;
    end;
    procedure CheckForEmptyLoc;      {Checks to see if the next location is empty.}
    begin
        FoundEmptyLoc := false;
        TablePos := TablePos + 1;
        if Table[TablePos] = -1 then
            begin
                FoundEmptyLoc :=  true;
                Table[TablePos] := DataItem
            end;
    end;
    procedure CreateTable;                {Sets up the table of data items.}
    begin
        writeln('Data items consist of 1 to 4 digits only');
        writeln;
        write('How many items do you wish to enter? ');
        readln(Count);
        for x := 1 to Count do
            begin
                write('Enter data item number ',x,' ');
                readln(DataItem);
                TablePos := DataItem mod TableSize; {Simple Hashing Formula}
                if TablePos = 0 then      {Put item at bottom of table.}
                    TablePos := TableSize;
                if Table[TablePos] = -1 then
                    Table[TablePos] := DataItem
                else
                    begin
                        if TablePos = TableSize then {Start at top of table.}
                            TablePos := 0;
                        repeat
                            CheckForEmptyLoc;
                        until (FoundEmptyLoc) or (TablePos = TableSize);
                        if not FoundEmptyLoc then
```

```
                        begin
                            TablePos : = 0;
                            repeat
                                    CheckForEmptyLoc;
                            until (FoundEmptyLoc);
                        end;
                    end;
            end;
end;
procedure CheckIfFound;      {Checks current item to see if it is the requested one.}
begin
    if ItemToBeFound = Table[TablePos] then
        begin
            FoundPos : = TablePos;
            ItemFound : = true;
        end;
end;
procedure FindDataItem;      {Searches the list to find a given item.}
var
    reply : char;
begin
    repeat
        ItemFound : = false;
        write('Enter the data item to be searched for ');
        readln(ItemToBeFound);
        TablePos : = ItemToBeFound mod TableSize; {Same Hashing Formula as before}
        if TablePos = 0 then                      {Try item at bottom of table.}
            TablePos : = TableSize;
        CheckIfFound;
        if not ItemFound then
            begin
                if TablePos = TableSize then  {Restart search at top of table.}
                    TablePos : = 0;
                repeat
                    TablePos : = TablePos + 1;
                    CheckIfFound;
                until ItemFound or (TablePos = TableSize);
                if not ItemFound then
                    begin
                        TablePos : = 0;
                        repeat
```

```
                                TablePos : = TablePos + 1;
                                CheckIfFound;
                            until ItemFound or (TablePos = TableSize);
                        end;
                end;
                if ItemFound then
                    writeln(ItemToBeFound,' located at position ',FoundPos)
                else
                    writeln('Item is not in the list');
                writeln;
                write('Do you wish to search for another item? ');
                readln(reply);
                writeln;
            until (reply = 'n') or (reply = 'N');
    end;
    begin          {The main body of program}
        EmptyTheTable;
        CreateTable;
        DisplayTable;
        FindDataItem;
    end.
```

Many different types of hashing formulas are to be found; exercise number 2 at the end of this chapter describes a technique for hashing names into a table.

Data Structures

Arrays and records are examples of data structures that come, ready to use, with Pascal. There are, however, occasions when the programmer needs to use data structures that are not readily available. This section concentrates on two of the most commonly-used data structures: the *stack* and the *queue*. Complete programs are supplied to demonstrate these data structures.

Stacks

A *stack* is a *last in first out* (or *lifo*) data structure. This means that the last item of data to be placed on the stack will be the first item of data that can be removed from the stack. As data is entered it is placed onto the top of the stack; a process called *pushing* the stack, and when data is removed it is taken from the top of the stack; a process called *popping* the stack. Thus, data can only be *pushed* and *popped* using the top of the stack.

To keep track of where the top of the stack currently is, that is, the location of the top of the stack, a *stack pointer* is used; this is a variable (called *StackPtr* in the program below) which contains a number representing the position of the item stored on the top of the stack. The contents of the stack pointer are updated whenever an item is added to or removed from the stack. The stack pointer is *incremented* (increased by 1) whenever an item is pushed onto the stack and is *decremented* (decreased by 1) whenever an item is popped from the stack. An attempt to push data onto a full stack results in *stack overflow* and an attempt to pop data from an empty stack results in *stack underflow*.

The bottom, or *base* of the stack, is fixed at position 1 and the stack has an upper limit beyond which items cannot be stored. The program below allows 10 items to be stored on the stack and so the upper limit is 10. This is declared using a constant called *StackLimit*; for a larger or smaller stack simply alter the value of this constant.

The diagrams below illustrate the operation of the stack.

(1)   An empty stack.

The stack contains no data and the stack pointer (*StackPtr*) indicates this by containing the value 0. The program uses this fact in the condition it uses to check for an empty stack. In this state, data can only be pushed onto the stack, and an attempt to pop the stack will result in an error message being displayed, namely *Warning! Stack Underflow*.

Data	Stack Position	StackPtr Value = 0 (Top of Stack)
	10	
	9	
	8	
	7	
	6	
	5	
	4	
	3	
	2	
	1	Stack Base = Position 1
	(0)	⟵——— *StackPtr*

(2)   A full stack.

The stack is completely filled with data; the condition for this is that the *StackPtr* value is equal to the *StackLimit* value of 10. In this state, data can only be popped from the stack. If an attempt is made to push data onto the stack, an error message will be displayed, namely *Warning! Stack Overflow*.

Data	Stack Position	StackPtr Value = 10 (Top of Stack)
5	10	⟵——— *StackPtr*
3	9	
5	8	
6	7	
8	6	
9	5	
1	4	
2	3	
4	2	
7	1	Stack Base = Position 1

(3)   A non-empty, non-full stack.

Here, the stack contains 6 items, so the StackPtr value is equal to 6. In this state, the stack can either be popped or pushed.

Data	Stack Position	
		StackPtr Value = 6 (Top of Stack)
	10	
	9	
	8	
	7	
8	6	←——— StackPtr
9	5	
1	4	
2	3	
4	2	
7	1	Stack Base = Position 1

If two data items were now removed, the state of the stack would be as shown below:

Data	Stack Position	
		StackPtr Value = 4 (Top of Stack)
	10	
	9	
	8	
	7	
	6	
	5	
1	4	←——— StackPtr
2	3	
4	2	
7	1	Stack Base = Position 1

The program to illustrate the action of this stack is called StackSimulation and is written in standard Pascal with the exception of the use of the *random* function (see section on miscellaneous functions) which is used to produce numbers to be entered onto the stack. This saves the user from having to type them in, which is a tedious business. In *StackSimulation*, when numbers are popped from the stack they are simply discarded; in an actual application the numbers would need to be transferred to some destination (or variable) in order to be used.

The program is menu-driven; the user is presented with a choice of either *pushing* the stack, *popping* the stack, *resetting* the stack or *quitting* the program. After each operation has been carried out, with the exception of *quit*, the menu is re-displayed.

```
program StackSimulation (input, output);
const
      StackLimit = 10;          {Stack holds 10 numbers at most.}
var
      stack : array[1..StackLimit] of integer;
      StackPtr : integer;
procedure DisplayStack;         {Displays the contents of the stack.}
```

```
var
    x : integer;
begin
    writeln;
    for x := 1 to StackLimit do
        write(stack[x]:6);
    writeln;
    writeln;
    writeln('Stack Pointer Value is now ',StackPtr);
end;
procedure ResetStack;{Sets every stack location to 0.}
var
    x : integer;
begin
    writeln;
    for x := 1 to StackLimit do
        stack[x] := 0;
    StackPtr := 0;
    DisplayStack;
end;
procedure push;        {Pushes a data item (random number) onto the stack.}
                       {If the stack is full, a warning message is displayed.}
begin
    if StackPtr < StackLimit then
        begin
            StackPtr := StackPtr + 1;{Increment the stack pointer.}
            stack[StackPtr] := random(9) + 1;
        end
    else
        begin
            writeln;
            writeln('Warning! Stack overflow');
        end;
    DisplayStack;
end;
procedure pop;        {Pops a data item from the stack.}
                      {If the stack is empty, a warning message is displayed.}
begin
    if StackPtr > 0 then
        begin
            stack[StackPtr] := 0;{This is just to show that it has been removed}
```

```
                StackPtr : = StackPtr — 1;{Decrement the stack pointer.}
                DisplayStack;
            end
        else
            begin
                writeln;
                writeln('Warning! Stack underflow');
                DisplayStack;
            end;
    end;
    procedure menu;       {Displays a menu to show the user}
                          {the choices that are available.}
    begin
        writeln;
        writeln('Do you wish to    (1) Push an item onto the stack?');
        writeln('                  (2) Pop an item from the stack?');
        writeln('                  (3) Reset the stack?');
        writeln('                  (4) Quit the program?');
    end;
    procedure UserChoice;          {Finds out which operation the user requires}
                                   {and calls up the appropriate procedure.}

    var
        reply : char;
    begin
        repeat
            menu;
            readln(reply);
            if reply = '1' then
                push;
            if reply = '2' then
                pop;
            if reply = '3' then
                ResetStack;
        until reply = '4';
    end;
    begin{Main body of program.}
        randomize;
        ResetStack;
        UserChoice;
    end.
```

Queues

A queue operates in a similar fashion to a stack but with the difference that data is always added to the rear of a queue and is always removed from the front of a queue; with a stack, remember, data is inserted and removed at the same point - the top of the stack.

This means that a queue requires two pointers; one (called *rear*) to indicate the position of the rear of the queue, the other (called *front*) to indicate the position of the front of the queue. *Front* will always indicate the position of the first data item in the queue and *rear* will always indicate the *next free* position at the rear of the queue, rather than the last data item in the queue. As we shall see shortly, this will enable us to distinguish between a full queue and an empty queue.

A queue of this kind operates quite like a queue waiting at a supermarket cash-out except that our queue does not move forward when a data item has been removed. The reason for this is simply that there is no need; the front pointer always keeps track of the position of the front of the queue, and also, given the fact that a queue like this could contain millions of data items, moving the queue physically forward could turn out to be a very time-consuming operation.

Another feature of our queue is that when the available positions at the rear of the queue have been used up, it is possible for the queue to 'wrap around' to the front and use any vacant positions there. Once again, our pointers will be used to keep track of the positions of the front and the rear of the queue.

We are now in a position to write down the conditions that are required in order to recognize when a queue is empty and when a queue is full.

A queue is empty when

    front = rear

that is, when both pointers point to the same position, and a queue is full when either

    (rear = front − 1)

or,

    (front = 1) and (rear = QueueLimit).

Note that when the queue is full there must always be one location left empty; without this we would not be able to write down such simple conditions for distinguishing a full queue from an empty one.

Some examples are given below to clarify the points made; note that empty locations are identified by 'filling' them with 0's, whereas occupied locations contain one digit in the range 1 to 9.

(1)   An empty queue, before being reset. The last item to be removed from the queue was in position 3. After it was removed the front pointer was incremented thus giving the condition *front = rear*, signifying an empty queue.

Position	1	2	3	4	5	6	7	8	9	10
	0	0	0	0	0	0	0	0	0	0

front = 4
rear = 4

(2)   An empty queue that has been reset. The front and rear pointers have been initialized to 1.

Position	1	2	3	4	5	6	7	8	9	10
	0	0	0	0	0	0	0	0	0	0

front = 1
rear = 1

(3)   A non-empty, non-full queue that has not wrapped around. The next item to join the queue will be entered in position 8, the next item to leave the queue will be the item in position 3.

Position	1	2	3	4	5	6	7	8	9	10
	0	0	2	5	6	3	9	0	0	0

front = 3   rear = 8

(4)   A non-empty, non-full queue that has wrapped around. This is the result of removing two items and adding four items to the queue shown in example (3) above.

Position	1	2	3	4	5	6	7	8	9	10
	8	0	0	0	6	3	9	4	2	7

rear = 2   front = 5

(5)   A full queue that has not wrapped around, identified by the condition (*front* = 1) *and* (*rear* = *QueueLimit*). The locations from 1 to 9 are filled and no more items can be added to the queue since the rear pointer would wrap around and point to position 1. This would give the condition for an empty queue.

Position	1	2	3	4	5	6	7	8	9	10
	8	1	5	7	6	3	9	4	2	0

front = 1   rear = 10

(6)   A full queue that has wrapped around, easily identified by the condition *rear* = *front* – 1.

Position	1	2	3	4	5	6	7	8	9	10
	8	1	5	7	0	3	9	4	2	7

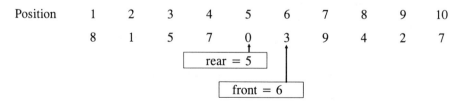

rear = 5

front = 6

A program to simulate the action of this queue is given below; it follows the style of the previous stack program and uses random numbers to simulate data items joining the queue.

```
program QueueSimulation (input, output);
const
        QueueLimit = 10;        {Sets the size of the queue to 10.}
                                {Alter this value if you wish.}
var
        queue : array[1..QueueLimit] of integer;
        front, rear, x : integer;
procedure DisplayQueue;        {Displays the queue and its pointer values}
                                {on the monitor.}
begin
    writeln;
    for x : = 1 to QueueLimit do
        write(queue[x],' ');
    writeln;
    writeln('front =',front,' rear =',rear);
end;
procedure ResetQueue;        {'Fills' the queue with 0's and sets front and rear}
                                {pointers to 1.}
begin
    for x : = 1 to QueueLimit do
        queue[x] : = 0;
    front : = 1;
    rear : = 1;
end;
procedure AddItem; {Adds a data item to the queue and adjusts pointers.}
begin
    if front = rear then
        ResetQueue;
    if not((rear = front − 1) or ((front = 1) and (rear = QueueLimit))) then
        begin{Make sure the queue is not full.}
            queue[rear] : = random(9) + 1;
            if rear = QueueLimit then
                rear : = 1 {Wrap pointer around to front of queue.}
            else
                rear : = rear + 1; {Increment the rear pointer.}
            DisplayQueue;
        end
    else
        begin {Warn user that the queue is full.}
```

```
                    writeln;
                    writeln('WARNING! Queue is full. Cannot add a data item');
                    DisplayQueue;
                end;
        end;
    procedure RemoveItem; {Removes a data item from the queue and adjusts pointers.}
    begin
        if front < > rear then
            begin {Make sure the queue is not empty.}
                queue[front] : = 0;{This is just to show that it has been removed}
                if front = QueueLimit then
                    front : = 1 {Wrap pointer around to front of queue.}
                else
                    front : = front + 1; {Increment the front pointer.}
                DisplayQueue;
                if front = rear then
                    ResetQueue; {Queue is empty, so reset it.}
            end
        else
            begin {Warn user that the queue is empty.}
                writeln;
                writeln('WARNING! Queue is empty. Cannot remove a data item');
                DisplayQueue;
            end;
    end;
    procedure menu; {Displays options available to the user.}
    begin
        writeln;
        writeln('Do you wish to  (1) Add an item to the queue?');
        writeln('                (2) Remove an item from the queue?');
        writeln('                (3) Reset the queue?');
        writeln('                (4) Quit the program?');
    end;
    procedure UserChoice;       {Determines user's choice}
                                {and calls up appropriate procedure.}
    var
        reply:char;
    begin
        repeat
            menu;
            readln(reply);
```

```
        if reply = '1' then
            AddItem;
        if reply = '2' then
            RemoveItem;
        if reply = '3' then
            begin
                ResetQueue;
                DisplayQueue;
            end;
    until reply = '4';
end;
begin {Main body of program.}
    randomize;
    ResetQueue;
    DisplayQueue;
    UserChoice;
end.
```

Re-Usable Components

Throughout this book, global variables have been used extensively in the demonstration programs. There is nothing really wrong with this, except that any procedures or functions that were created in these programs probably relied upon some, or all, of the global variables that were declared at the start of the programs. Should we wish to use one of these procedures or functions in another program, then we will probably have to change the names of some, or all, of its variables in order to match those used in the new program. Alternatively, we may have to change the names of some of the variables in the new program.

This makes procedures and functions difficult to copy. Ideally, we should be writing procedures and functions that can be used in any program without needing to be modified; in other words we should be producing *re-usable components*. Procedures and functions should become components that we can just 'plug' into programs whenever they are needed. The standard functions and procedures supplied with Pascal are examples of such components; we use them without having any knowledge of the variable or constant names or the code used inside of them.

The way to produce re-usable components is to use parameters (variable or otherwise) in all of our procedures or functions which require values to be passed to them when they are called. All other variables, for loop control, counting etc., can be declared locally inside the procedure or function.

To illustrate this, recall the stack program given earlier in this chapter. An array to hold the stack, and a stackpointer to keep track of the top of the stack, were declared globally and then used in the procedures for pushing, popping and resetting the stack. This was fine for one stack but what would happen if we wanted to manipulate two stacks (stack1 and stack2 for example) in the same program? We would have to copy the stack routines so that one set of procedures would manipulate stack1 and the other set would manipulate stack2. This is very wasteful of code and also time-consuming.

The program below, called TwoStacks, illustrates the use of re-usable components. Each stack procedure is now 'stand-alone' in that it does not rely on global variables for its operation. Note, however, the use of a global constant to define the size of each stack and a type used to define the structure of each stack; these are used to ensure compatibility of the stacks used in the program with the procedures used to manipulate them.

```
program TwoStacks (input, output);
const
    StackLimit = 10;{Stack holds 10 numbers at most.}
type
    StackType = array[1..StackLimit] of integer;
var
    stack1, stack2 : StackType;   {The stacks to be manipulated}
    StackPtr1, StackPtr2 : integer;           {and their associated pointers.}
procedure DisplayStack(var stack : StackType; var StackPtr : integer);
                                  {Displays the contents of a stack.}
var
    x : integer;
begin
    writeln;
    for x := 1 to StackLimit do
        write(stack[x]:6);
    writeln;
    writeln;
    writeln('Stack Pointer Value is now ',StackPtr);
end;
procedure ResetStack (var stack : StackType; var StackPtr : integer);
{Sets every stack location to 0.}
var
    x : integer;
begin
    writeln;
    for x := 1 to StackLimit do
        stack[x] := 0;
    StackPtr := 0;
    DisplayStack (stack, StackPtr);
end;
procedure push       (var stack :StackType; var StackPtr : integer);
                     {Pushes a data item (random number) onto a stack.}
                     {If stack is full, a warning message is displayed.}
begin
    if StackPtr < StackLimit then
        begin
```

```
                StackPtr : = StackPtr + 1;{Increment the stack pointer.}
                stack[StackPtr] : = random(9) + 1;
            end
        else
            begin
                writeln;
                writeln('Warning! Stack overflow');
            end;
        DisplayStack(stack, StackPtr);
end;
procedure pop (var stack : StackType; var StackPtr : integer);
                {Pops a data item from a stack.}
                {If stack is empty, a warning message is displayed.}
begin
    if StackPtr > 0 then
        begin
            stack[StackPtr] : = 0;     {This is just to show that it has been removed}
            StackPtr : = StackPtr — 1;         {Decrement the stack pointer.}
            DisplayStack(stack, StackPtr);
        end
    else
        begin
            writeln;
            writeln('Warning! Stack underflow');
            DisplayStack(stack, StackPtr);
        end;
end;
procedure UserChoice;        {Finds out which stack & which operation required}
                            {and calls up the appropriate procedure.}
var
    reply : char;
    StackNumber : integer;
begin
    repeat
        writeln;
        write('Which stack — (1 or 2)?');
        readln(StackNumber);
        writeln;
        writeln('Do you wish to (1) Push an item onto this stack?');
        writeln('              (2) Pop an item from this stack?');
        writeln('              (3) Reset this stack?');
```

```
            writeln('                    (4) Quit the program?');
            readln(reply);
            if StackNumber = 1 then
                begin
                    if reply = '1' then
                            push(stack1, StackPtr1);
                    if reply = '2' then
                            pop(stack1, StackPtr1);
                    if reply = '3' then
                            ResetStack(stack1, StackPtr1);
                end
            else
                begin
                    if reply = '1' then
                            push(stack2, StackPtr2);
                    if reply = '2' then
                            pop(stack2, StackPtr2);
                    if reply = '3' then
                            ResetStack(stack2, StackPtr2);
                end;
            until reply = '4';
    end;
    begin          {Main body of program.}
        randomize;
        ResetStack(stack1, StackPtr1);
        ResetStack(stack2, StackPtr2);
        UserChoice; {Simple interactive user procedure to control the stacks.}
    end.
```

Exercises

1   The hash table method employed in this chapter searched down the table look-
    ing for an empty location if it was found that the address calculated by the
    hashing algorithm was occupied. Devise an alternative strategy to overcome
    this problem. You need not write a program to implement your strategy!

2   If your version of Pascal supports the data type *string*, adapt the hash table
    program in the text so that it will store, and then retrieve, *names* rather than
    numbers. A hashing algorithm to accomplish this could include the following
    steps (or you could devise your own):

    (a)   Extract the first letter of the name to be stored (or retrieved)

    (b)   Using appropriate functions, calculate the *position* of this letter in the
          alphabet, for example, 'a' = 1, 'b' = 2, 'c' = 3, etc.

(c) Multiply the *position* value by the size of the table (for example, *TableSize* could be 25 or 50. See the hashing program in the text.) and then divide this result by 26 (because there are 26 letters in the alphabet).

For example, given a hash table which can store 50 names and we wish to enter the name 'colin'; the first letter, 'c', would be extracted (using a statement such as *FirstLetter := name[1]*) and then its alphabetic position, (in this case, 3), would be determined by applying the *ord* function to *FirstLetter* and then subtracting 95. This value (3) would then be multiplied by 50 (the table size), giving 150 and then the 150 would be divided by 26 (using *div*) yielding the integer result of 5.

3 (a) Using your hashing program from question 2, add extra code to calculate the average *search length* of this hashing method, that is, when searching for an item in the table, how many data items, on average, must be examined until the required one is located. Run this program with a half-filled table and then with a completely filled table. Comment on your results.

(b) Use a *binary search* with 50 names and calculate the average search length and maximum search length for this. Compare with the results in part (a).

N.B. If your version of Pascal does not support the type *string* do this exercise using numerical data instead of character string data. (You can adapt the programs provided in the text to calculate the search lengths.)

4 Refer to the program *SalesMen*. Write a procedure to read the sales file stored on disk and store it in an array so that it can be examined. Also, add new code to the procedure *AmendSalesData* in *SalesMen* so that validation checks are carried out on the salesman's number and the week number before an amendment is attempted.

Assignment

Write a package to manipulate matrices of size 2 × 2. That is, matrices such as:

$$\begin{bmatrix} 1 & 4 \\ 12 & 5 \end{bmatrix} \quad \text{and} \quad \begin{bmatrix} 12 & 7 \\ 11 & -3 \end{bmatrix}$$

The user options required are:

(1) Add two matrices

(2) Subtract two matrices

(3) Multiply two matrices

(4) Find the inverse of a matrix

(5) Quit

Notes

Adding the matrices

$$\begin{bmatrix} a & b \\ c & d \end{bmatrix} \quad \text{and} \quad \begin{bmatrix} e & f \\ g & h \end{bmatrix}$$

produces the matrix

$$\begin{bmatrix} a+e & b+f \\ c+g & d+h \end{bmatrix}$$

Subtracting the matrices

$$\begin{bmatrix} a & b \\ c & d \end{bmatrix} \quad \text{and} \quad \begin{bmatrix} e & f \\ g & h \end{bmatrix}$$

produces the matrix

$$\begin{bmatrix} a-e & b-f \\ c-g & d-h \end{bmatrix}$$

Multiplying the matrices

$$\begin{bmatrix} a & b \\ c & d \end{bmatrix} \quad \text{and} \quad \begin{bmatrix} e & f \\ g & h \end{bmatrix}$$

produces the matrix

$$\begin{bmatrix} (a*e+b*g) & (a*f+b*h) \\ (c*e+d*g) & (c*f+d*h) \end{bmatrix}$$

The inverse of the matrix

$$\begin{bmatrix} a & b \\ c & d \end{bmatrix} \quad \text{is given by} \quad \begin{bmatrix} d/det & -b/det \\ -c/det & a/det \end{bmatrix}$$

where det (short for *determinant*) is given by $(a*d - b*c)$, and where a, b, c, d, e, f, g and h refer to the elements (that is, the numbers stored) in the matrices.

Appendix

The ASCII Code

Computers can only store data using binary patterns of 0's and 1's. In order to store characters some method of coding must be used. The code that is used most frequently nowadays is the American Standard Code for Information Interchange, normally referred to as the ASCII code for brevity. Each character is given a unique value in the ASCII code. For example 'a' has the code (in decimal) 97. Inside a computer, however, 'a' would be stored using the binary pattern 01100001. The code set is normally shown using decimal values because they are easier to relate to than binary patterns. A useful subset of the ASCII code is given below.

The codes 32 through to 125 are all character (or printable) codes:

32 <blank> or <space>	64 @	96
33 !	65 A	97 a
34 "	66 B	98 b
35 £	67 C	99 c
36 $	68 D	100 d
37 %	69 E	101 e
38 &	70 F	102 f
39 ' (quote)	71 G	103 g
40 (	72 H	104 h
41)	73 I	105 i
42 *	74 J	106 j
43 +	75 K	107 k
44 , (comma)	76 L	108 l
45 –	77 M	109 m
46 . (full stop)	78 N	110 n
47 /	79 O	111 o
48 0	80 P	112 p
49 1	81 Q	113 q
50 2	82 R	114 r
51 3	83 S	115 s
52 4	84 T	116 t
53 5	85 U	117 u
54 6	86 V	118 v
55 7	87 W	119 w
56 8	88 X	120 x
57 9	89 Y	121 y
58 :	90 Z	122 z
59 ;	91 [	123 {
60 <	92	124
61 =	93]	125 }
62 >	94 ^	
63 ?	95	

The first 32 codes (0 to 31) are called control (or non-printable) codes because they cause some action to be taken other than the printing of a character. The useful ones to know are:

8 Backspace	9 Horizontal Tab	10 Line Feed
12 Form Feed	13 Carriage Return	27 Escape

Index

Other computer textbooks from Business Education Publishers

Information Processing
Third Edition

Geoffrey Knott   Nick Waites
August 1997   352 pp
ISBN 0 907679 97 8 Soft Cover £15.95

The new edition of this popular text demonstrates the importance of computerised Information Processing in modern organisations. The text has been extensively revised to keep students aware of the most recent changes and developments. It assumes no previous knowledge of the subject and is suitable for National, Advanced, Higher National and undergraduate programmes which have an Information Processing requirement. Business, Finance and Management courses will find the text highly relevant. The text also meets the requirements of Members of the Association of Accountancy Technicians (AAT), who are studying for Paper 6, Elements of Information Systems.

Each chapter is followed by exercises designed to test the reader's retention of facts and understanding of ideas developed within the text.

A programme of 25 problem-based assignments provides assessment coverage of all the topics in the book and could form the basis of a teaching programme. Each assignment indicates the chapters which are of particular use for its completion.

Small Business Computer Systems
Second Edition

Geoffrey Knott   March 1994   284 pp
ISBN 0 907679 60 9 Soft Cover £14.50

This text covers the Small Business Computer Systems stream of BTEC courses and is also ideal for undergraduates and HNC/HND students of any discipline and for professionals who require a fundamental understanding of microcomputer technology and applications. It provides students with a wealth of source material and the programme of problem based assignments is designed to consolidate students' learning at every stage.

The second edition extensively updates the material provided in the first, and reflects the most recent developments in microcomputer hardware and software.

Microcomputer users and practitioners, in both the small business and corporate fields, will find the book a highly readable and invaluable resource.

Computing
Second Edition

Nick Waites Geoffrey Knott
September 1996   768 pp
ISBN 0 907679 87 0   Size 252 x 200mm
Soft Cover   £16.95

The text has been specifically designed to cover the Advanced Level Computing syllabuses of the major examining boards. It is also highly suitable for students of first year BTEC HNC/HND courses in computing and Part 1 of the British Computer Society. Examination practice is provided through a range of actual examination questions selected from a number of major examining boards. A Tutor's Manual containing suggested solutions is available from the Publisher for centres which adopt the book.

A disk produced by Microfile, the educational software house, containing software to supplement a number of selected topics from the text, can be purchased from the Publishers. The disk includes an integrated suite of programs for an assembler specifically designed for educational use, a number of programs to illustrate data structures and the source listings of a number of sorting programs described in the book.

GCSE Information Systems
Nick Waites

August 1994 320 pp ISBN 0 907679 71 4
Size 252 x 200mm   Soft Cover £11.50

GCSE Information Systems has been written specifically for the National Curriculum Attainment Target 5: Information Technology Capability.

The material presented in the book covers the syllabus extensions for students who wish to obtain a GCSE in Information Systems.

The text, which covers all aspects of information technology and information systems, includes:

- basic computer operation principles
- hardware devices
- the different types of software
- problem solving techniques
- elements of programming in BASIC, Pascal and Logo
- systems analysis and design
- applications of computers
- social issues relating to computers
- glossary of commonly used computing terms

The text is supplemented with numerous diagrams and self-test questions and answers are provided at the end of each chapter. A number of model GCSE examination questions have also been included. These features combine to provide an excellent general introduction to computing for GCSE students or for people who out of interest, simply wish to learn more about this important subject.